Complete
HORSE
Book

Complete
HORSE
Book

General Editor: Peter Roberts

admiral

CONTENTS

LOOKING AT THE HORSE	6
How the Horse Evolved	8
Horses in the Wild	18
Principal Breeds	28
HORSE AND RIDER	50
Buying a Horse	52
Horse Equipment	60
Training the Horse	74
The Rider	88
Keep and Care	108
Medical Matters	122
HORSES IN ACTION	134
The Working Horse	136
The Sporting Horse	146
The Olympians	162
The Spanish Riding School of Vienna	180
GLOSSARY	188
INDEX	190

This book was devised and produced by
Multimedia Publications (UK) Ltd

Editor: Richard Rosenfeld
Assistant Editor: Sydney Francis
Design: Behram Kapadia
Picture Research: Irene Lynch
Illustrations: Janos Marffy

Copyright © Multimedia Publications (UK) Ltd 1985

First published in the United Kingdom 1985 by Admiral Books an
imprint owned jointly by W H Smith and Son Limited, Registered No
237811, England, trading as WHS Distributors, St John's House, East
Street, Leicester LE1 6NE and Multimedia Publications (UK)
Limited, Central House, 1 Ballards Lane, London N3 1UZ.

ISBN 1 85171 007 8

Typeset by Flowery Typesetters Ltd, London
Origination by D.S. Colour International Ltd, London.
Printed in Italy by Poligrafici Calderara S.p.a., Bologna

Left: J. Whittaker and Singing
Wind clear a fence at Hickstead.

Endpapers: Horses are naturally
affectionate animals.

Page 1: Thick, shaggy coats help
to insulate against the cold.

Pages 2-3: Hungarian
Thoroughbreds demonstrate that
"the grass is always greener on
the other side of the fence"

LOOKING AT THE HORSE

وتحلل القنص والجمالة والقنص والبذلة انها لضغت علي بالله فأضاعت بقض مزرجها

فنشد مزرجها فلما دانني وتمنت بالرقعة درهما وقطعة وقلت لها ان رغبت في المشوف المعلم

واشرت الي الدرهم فوجي بالسر المهم وان ابن ان نرجي فخذي القطعة وابيرحن

فان الي استخلاض البدر بالنزم والابلج الهمم وقالت دع جدالك وبلغ عما بدا لك فأسطع

طلع الشيخ وبلده والشعر وناسج برداته فقالت ان الشيخ من أهل ضاروج وهو الذي وتنا

HOW THE HORSE EVOLVED

While the horse plays a part in almost every aspect of man's history, his own history began millions and millions of years before man evolved. An amazing record of fossilized remains has enabled paleontologists to trace the horse back to the Eocene period of prehistory, a period that extended from roughly 60 million to 40 million years ago. In the warm, moist atmosphere of this era, there emerged among the welter of plant and animal life flourishing at the time a creature that few people would recognize as being the first recorded ancestor of today's horses and ponies.

The Dawn Horse

Known scientifically as *Hyracotherium* or *Eohippus*, and more romantically as the "dawn horse", his size and shape were probably more those of a large dog. From the base of his neck to the ground he measured about 15 in (37 cm) and he had a small head with short ears and a tapering muzzle. His back was curved and rounded, his tail long, thin and bony, and he had three toes on the hind feet and four on the front.

Unlike a dog, however, he was a herbivore, not a carnivore, but even in this he was not wholly like today's horse, for he was a browser, not a grazer. The shape of his teeth indicate that his diet consisted of the succulent leaves of the tropical vegetation, not the tough grass of the plains.

Eohippus inhabited the land mass of North America and it is from here that the most prolific fossil finds have been made. But because those areas of the world long since identified as Europe and Asia were still joined to the Americas by land rather than separated by oceans, *Eohippus* was able to wander across to inhabit these places too.

Eohippus was, therefore, the first animal recognizable to naturalists and paleontologists as the ancestor of the horse, but there were to be many links in the evolutionary chain before he emerged as the animal we know today.

Left: In this thirteenth-century Arabic illumination from the Maqamat of Al-Hariri, the standard-bearers of the Caliph are all mounted on horses, while the drummer rides an ass.

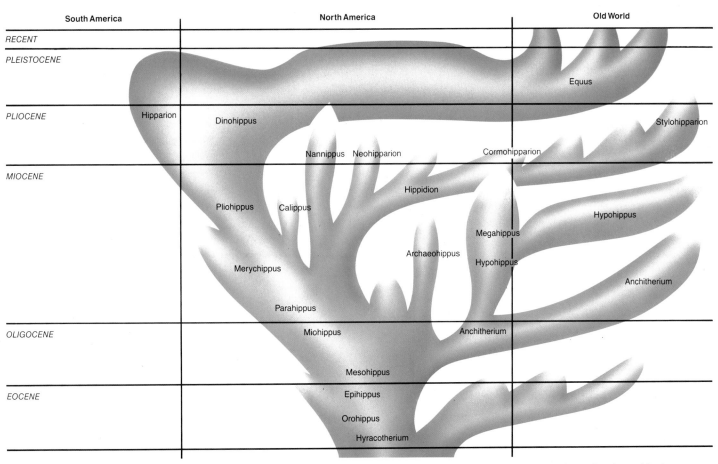

Hyracotherium, the earliest form of the horse, appeared approximately 55 million years ago. This illustration shows the various stages of its evolution through the Oligocene, Miocene, Pliocene and Pleistocene periods to the present day.

Above: Man's-eye view of the first horses. This detail from the cave paintings at Lascaux, France, is an early record of the prehistoric horse.

Left: Equus Przewalskii has remained virtually unchanged since the Ice Age. It is generally considered to be the only true wild horse remaining as it has never, at any stage in history, been tamed by man. A herd of these ponies was discovered in Mongolia at the end of the last century by the Russian explorer Colonel Przewalski (hence the name). Small numbers of Przewalski's Horses still live in the Mongolian steppes, and a herd is kept in Prague zoo.

Recognizable ancestor

As the earth underwent the changes that have made it possible to separate the huge time scale of prehistory into various epochs, so animals had to change too, in order to adapt to altered conditions. Thus *Eohippus* was followed by *Orohippus*, then *Epihippus*, *Mesohippus* and *Miohippus*, *Parahippus*, *Merychippus* and *Pliohippus*. *Pliohippus* emerged during the Pliocene period which dates from ten to one million years BC, and by this time he was quite definitely recognizable as the ancestor of the modern horse.

The changes apparent in each of these prehistoric "horses" came about, as suggested, to adapt to the changing surroundings. As the great tropical jungles were washed away and their place taken by the drier, grassy plains, so the teeth of the horse's ancestors changed in order to cope with the tough grass that became their diet. In the jungles he had the protection of thicker vegetation in which to hide from predators, and was nimble enough to spring away when danger came too close.

As the open grassy plains became his feeding grounds, however, he had to be able to move faster, for, being a non-aggressive animal, he was forced to make his escape by speed, by being able to run quicker than those animals that would prey upon him. The limbs of each emerging new species became progressively longer, the bones more powerful, the back straighter – and the speed greater.

Toe to hoof

The toes on the feet of little *Eohippus* were adapted to the marshy ground that typified the Eocene period. As time went on and land conditions changed, so the toes gradually retracted. Firstly the fourth toe became vestigial so that the four-toed browsing *Eohippus* gave way to the three-toed grazing *Mesohippus*. Then the lateral toes began to retract until they no longer came into contact with the ground. The middle toe was surrounded by a horn cap, adapting it for speedy movement over the firmer ground. *Pliohippus* was among the first of nature's true monodactyl (one-toed) creatures.

Pliohippus, it seems, sired a number of strains of primeval horse, none of which was to survive the ensuing Pleistocene period in North and South America. The reasons for this sudden extinction of the primeval horse in the New World have never been satisfactorily explained. Somehow it seems all the more strange, in that not only have the fossil remains of all the ancestors of the modern horse been found in greatest abundance in the Americas, but some of the early species have been found only there.

Equus Caballus

The most notable survivor of the horse-like creatures sired by *Pliohippus* is *Equus Caballus*, a progenitor of the modern horse. His bones have been found in North America but he disappeared there at some stage during the Pleistocene period (one million to 8150 BC) in which he emerged, and flourished in Europe, Asia and Africa. As man evolved and inhabited the earth, those who lived in the New World – the area which had undoubtedly been the cradle of the horse's ancestors – were not to see horses until they were frightened by the ones brought to that continent by the Spanish conquistadores in the sixteenth century AD.

Few animals in existence today can be traced with such comprehension back through the ages of prehistory to the dawn of their creation as can the horse. The rich collection of fossils making this possible was amassed during the mid-nineteenth century around the time that the world was reverberating from the shock of Charles Darwin's shattering theory of evolution. Not a few cynics were helped towards a grudging acceptance of, and belief in, his theories through these fossil records of the horse's ancestors.

Right: This terracotta figure from Cyprus, of a man armed with a shield astride a rather elongated horse, dates from 700-600 BC.

Above: The Syrians were one of the earliest civilizations to handle and ride horses. Here a Syrian knight in armor is pictured astride his charger, also adorned in battledress.

Living fossils

Up until the coming of *Equus Caballus,* experts seem much in agreement about the horse's evolution and passage through time. Thereafter, there is less agreement. Some people claim that all modern breeds of horse and pony are descended from just one type of primeval horse, that is directly from the descendants of *Equus Caballus. Equus Caballus,* it is claimed, can be seen "in the flesh" in a primitive pony still in existence today called *Equus Przewalskii.* A herd of these ponies was discovered in Mongolia at the end of the last century, by the Russian explorer after whom they were named and, in physical appearance, Przewalski's Horse seems to have remained virtually unchanged since the Ice Age.

Other experts in the development of the equine race disagree that the huge variety of types and breeds of horse and pony extant in the world today could have developed from just one basic species. Instead, they say, a number of wild horse species or types were responsible, but here there is further ground for disagreement, for the number of types, they argue, varies from two to six. Every theory is supportable by those who propound it, but so far agreement as to the indisputably correct one has been elusive. To us, the horse riders and handlers of today, it is probably not

important; what is perhaps of more interest, in view of our close relationship with the horse, is a look at man's early association with the animal, in order to trace some of the reasons for that relationship.

Man meets horse

It is certain that primitive man's first relationship with the horse was as a source of food – man hunted and killed the horse to eat. The very earliest cave paintings, such as those in the famous Lascaux caves in Southern France, depict the "hunt", and caches of horse bones split open with the marrow extracted found in Stone Age caves seem to endorse this aspect of the early association.

Early man and early horse were both nomads, wanderers in search of food. Horses lived together in the mutual protection of a herd, and the herd would wander from one grazing area to another. Man would follow, taking milk from the mares, and slaughtering members of the herd as necessary to provide food. It is not difficult to imagine that he began to make pets of the foals as time went on, just as we may assume that it was not long before he began to devise methods of using the horse – perhaps to help him in his nomadic existence, to pull some crude contraption along which would carry his meager belongings. Again, early cave paintings show that it did not take primitive man long to devise some form of halter, and to realize the value of sitting astride the horse, thus giving himself additional speed and elevation – definite advantages when hunting other beasts of the field.

Early riders

Just exactly when the horse was "domesticated" and by whom is still a little speculative. It is generally thought that either the Chinese or the Brahmans of India were the first to recognize the potential that lay in this animal. Evidence for the Chinese association comes from vases dating back to 3500 BC which depict the ridden and harnessed horse, while the Hindu religion of the Brahmins sets the first human astride a horse. Not long after this time, techniques of horsemanship and horsemastership were becoming widespread throughout Europe, North Africa and Asia – indeed everywhere that the horse was found.

There is evidence that well-known early civilizations – The Thracians, Hittites, Ionians, Sumerians, Assyrians, Phoenicians, Scythians, Parthians, Sybarites – all learnt to handle horses to a greater or lesser degree. The Parthians, for example, were such skilful horsemen that they could fire arrows at their enemies backwards as they appeared to be making a retreat.

Right: This beautifully engraved Etruscan urn has been decorated with a figure of Pegasus, the winged horse from Greek mythology, and Bellerophon, his tamer.

Dancing horses

The Sybarites taught their horses to "dance" – that is they had probably mastered some of the high school techniques recognized today as dressage. In fact, for the Sybarites this proved to be a disastrous idea. Their neighboring enemies, the Crotons, cleverly learned the tunes the Sybarites played to their horses, and began to play them in the thick of battle. The horses started "dancing" and their riders found themselves helpless to fight their enemies.

The Egyptians began their mastery of the horse in about 1600 BC, but initially they saw him as no more than a draft animal, used to pull the light, two-wheeled chariots that were the popular form of conveyance for both warfare and hunting. Riding was deemed fitting only for slaves and grooms. Surprisingly, the otherwise advanced Egyptians were way behind their neighbors, the Assyrians, who had perfected their techniques some thousand years earlier.

Myth and art

Evidence of the equestrian exploits of these early civilizations has come to us mainly through works of art and, to some extent, through mythological stories. That the horse figures so prominently in mythology from Central Europe to the Orient is evidence of the animal's enormous importance from earliest times.

Above left: This Greek urn, *circa* 340 BC, depicts the death of Hippolytus, torn apart when his horses were terrified by a monstrous bull.

Left: This mosaic of a man with his horse is still in its original position near the antiquarium in Carthage, Tunisia, and dates from the time of the Roman Empire.

Right: Ashurbanipal, an Assyrian king and warrior who ruled from 668-27 BC leading his horses in a relief dating from the seventh century BC.

In Greek mythology the horse was thought to have emerged from the sea as the creation of the water god, Poseidon. This myth may have started with invading armies that would bring their horses by ship, and ride them ashore in the shallow waters of the coast, appearing in a splash of spray from the ocean. It is probable that these invaders also gave rise to the myth of the centaur, half man and half horse, and perhaps to the famous winged horse of Greek mythology, Pegasus, whose name means "from the water".

In terms of art, the examples are legion. The very earliest records are those already mentioned – the cave paintings of primitive man. Later on the representation became more skilled; statuettes in stone, bronze and terracotta have been found from many ancient cultures. One of the earliest of these has been dated to 1000 BC and comes from Cyprus.

Later on, it was from reliefs and friezes showing the horse being used in hunting and in warfare that we learn more of its former history. The equestrian decorations on vases and burial urns from Iberia, China and Etrusca (to name but a few) have revealed valuable information, and proof of the importance of the horse's place in these cultures is also perhaps shown by the fine materials used; among them silver, ivory and delicate ceramic ware. Friezes, paintings, sculptures and mosaics depict the horse in use in ancient Rome, and the horsemen of the Pharaohs are shown in mosaics.

Even more significant, though, is the fact that horses were frequently depicted on early coins. Throughout the ages, it has been aspects of a civilization or important rulers – usually the rulers – that have been given this favored place.

Above: A detail from the famous Bayeux tapestry, showing a Norman rider being unseated from his blood-stained horse.

Left: Horses were often grazed on common land. In this detail from a thirteenth-century stained glass window from the Trinity Chapel, Canterbury, Richard Sunieve takes his master's horses out to pasture.

Right: This dramatic painting by Frederick Remington of Indians in the wild West rounding up wild horses hangs in the Cowboy Hall of Fame, Oklahoma.

Early documents

The first written document on horses comes from the Hittites and has been dated at about 1600 BC. Written in cuneiform on clay tablets, it talks of the care and rearing of horses. Coming much later in about 400 BC, but outstanding in its "modernity" is the written text of Xenophon, the great Greek poet and soldier. His *Treatise on Equitation* expounds the philosophy of horsemanship and the psychology of the horseman and horse, and experienced horsemen of today find little to argue with in its pages.

The early civilizations were constantly at war with one another: a major contributing factor in the spread of horses throughout Europe and Asia in those ancient times. Horses captured in battle would be turned out alongside those already indigenous to a given area, and differing strains would inevitably cross-breed.

Migration was also responsible for dissemination: many early tribesmen led nomadic lives, forced to stay on the move to find new grazing for their beasts and food for themselves. Not until primitive agricultural techniques were mastered could these people begin to settle permanently in one place.

Trading later took horses the length and breadth of the known world. The great silk and spice routes from China to the Mediterranean were used by traveling merchants and undoubtedly horses were exchanged with other items along the way.

Although little is known about horse breeds extant at this early time, it can be seen from the varying depictions of the animal in art that even then distinctly different types of horse existed in different parts of the world. In northern Europe the horse seems to have been rather coarse in appearance and covered with a thick coat, while those of the Orient or the desert lands of Asia Minor were lighter boned and finer in appearance, resembling the beautiful Arabian we know today. The notorious Mongol leader Genghis Khan and his "marauding hordes" swept through eastern lands 700 years ago on tough shaggy little ponies that looked similar in appearance to Przewalski's Horses.

It seems reasonable that completely different types of conditions bred different types of horses – adaptability to climate as much as anything else would decree this. However, as the horses crossed boundaries and became settled in new areas, they would mix with the other types of horses and, undoubtedly, cross-breeding took place. Some of it was perhaps even controlled by man, anxious from the earliest time to produce the best type of horse for himself. The horse breeds of today began to emerge, and, as time went on, man perfected the technique that nature has always practiced – that of selective breeding.

Round-up time for mares and foals. Each year herds of wild horses are rounded up for branding (to establish ownership) and for selling.

HORSES IN THE WILD

Man's domestication of the horse throughout the centuries has been so thorough and comprehensive that there are really no truly "wild" horses left in existence. This is not to say that there are no horses living in a wild state anywhere, unhelped or unhampered by man's intervention, for indeed there are. In the United States of America, in parts of Europe, Asia and Australia, horses roam uninhabited areas in small herds, living (more or less) the life of their wild ancestors. In many cases, however, these horses are the descendants of domesticated horses; the progeny of those animals who at some time and in some way escaped from the shackles of man's authority and headed back to the wide open spaces to live free. Such horses are more accurately termed feral, but it is as wild horses that they are generally known.

The life-cycle of all horses living free has a similar pattern, varying only according to the dictates of a particular area. Horses have no strong migratory habits as some wild animals do – their wanderings instead are dictated by hunger and thirst or the activities of hunters who pursue them. Generally, they live within a very small area. The wild horses of America, for example, in their heyday had a whole continent to call their own, but would usually graze over an area of no more than about 20 miles (30 kilometers) wide.

Being both non-aggressive and comparatively gregarious, horses in the wild generally live and move in a herd for mutual support and protection. At one time, herds would be huge, comprising many stallions and their harems; now, with the diminished numbers of wild horses, it is more usual to see only small bands of horses grazing together, and not necessarily with a stallion as their leader. It is probably the factors of living in the protection of a compact herd and within the confines of a relatively small area that are the main reasons for horses still being found living "wild" today, where in so many regions their habitat is being gradually eroded.

Below: Vast herds of Mustangs once roamed the prairies of North America, but many have been killed off in recent years. It is now a federal offence to kill wild horses.

American Mustangs

Among the most famous of all wild horses must surely be the Mustangs of the United States of America, horses which Frank J. Dobie, leading authority on their lives and habits, describes as "the most beautiful, the most spirited and the most inspiring creatures ever to print foot on the grasses of America". As we saw in the last chapter, while it seems likely that horses first evolved in North America, they vanished from that continent for a space of some million years, to be reintroduced by the Spanish Conqueror, Cortez, in the early 1500s when he landed in Mexico with just eleven stallions, five mares and a foal.

The horses Cortez brought with him were undoubtedly those that the Moors of Africa had used so successfully in their campaign to conquer the world for Islam – the Andalusian or Spanish Barb. The fact that these horses had not only survived what must have been a formidable sea crossing, but on landing were able to break their way through virgin wilderness while carrying loads of at least a quarter of their weight, gives some idea of their strength and stamina.

Above: In many parts of the world different breeds of wild horses and ponies are still to be found running free.

The conquistadores quickly established haciendas and ranches in order to produce more of these remarkable horses, and it is these animals that formed the basis of today's Mustangs. The name "Mustang" derives from the Spanish word for wild, *mestengo.*

The Mustang is perhaps most traditionally thought of as being the mount of the Indians of the Plains and the Southwest. Originally however the Indians were frightened by this animal they had never seen before – one that would allow a man to ride on its back. But their fear was soon conquered and they quickly began to appropriate horses for themselves, for status, for hunting and to ride into battle.

The Plains Indians were undoubtedly brilliant horsemen, but they were also a migratory people and careless herdsmen. As a result, countless numbers of horses escaped to live in the wild. Before long, the Mustang was scattered over an area that we can now define as eleven of the western states of the USA.

Returning to live as nature intended was not a problem for the Spanish Barb. His ancestors had lived and bred in freedom in the desert lands, so he was well used to shortages of water and food. As a result, Mustangs still thrive in their harsh habitat. They can go for days without food, and in arid conditions will chew at the prickly pear cactus to obtain moisture.

Today's Mustangs do not look very like their Spanish Barb ancestors. The Spanish Barb is a beautiful and majestic animal, strong-boned, broad-chested and impressive to look at. Adapting to life on those arid, inhospitable plains, however, has caused a certain degeneration in appearance, and the Mustang is small, somewhat inelegant and often even scraggy. Every coat color imaginable is seen, but undoubtedly the most famous are the piebald and skewbald "paint" horses that were so favored by the Indians.

Feral horses of the British isles

Great Britain is remarkable for its wealth of feral horses. Here the feral horses began their life as truly wild for in some cases they have been indigenous to the land since before man. There are nine breeds, every one of which still has its "wild" herds although all have domesticated relatives.

The breeds are the Connemara from the mounts of Galway and Mayo in the west of Ireland, the Welsh Mountain Pony, the Shetland from the Shetland Isles, the Highland also from Scotland, the Fells and Dales from the west and the east of the Pennine Hills in northern England respectively and the Exmoor, Dartmoor and New Forest, all of which take their names from the areas they inhabit in the South.

Below left: Ireland's native pony is the Connemara, a hardy breed that has roamed the hills of County Galway for centuries.

Above: The Spanish Barb can survive on meager rations.

Below: New Forest ponies grazing in their native habitat.

Above: Hardy Exmoor ponies are still to be found in large numbers roaming semi-wild over the heathery pastures of the Somerset and Devon moorlands.

The Welsh Mountain Pony has been roaming the Welsh Hills at least since Roman times, when it is said that Julius Caesar founded a stud in Merionethshire, while the Connemara is a descendant of a primitive pony that lived in the wilds of this area for centuries before man. This Irish pony has Spanish blood, either from Spanish horses that survived the shipwreck of the Spanish Armada and swam ashore in this area of Ireland or, more prosaically, from the trading that was conducted between the Spaniards and the merchants of Galway.

The tiny Shetland pony has been around since prehistoric times, although it is not known for sure how it got to the remote Shetland islands. Most probably both it and the bigger, stronger Highland ponies were taken to their wild homes by early man as he wandered the land.

The Exmoor pony is an ancient breed said to be the animal used by the Iron Age Celts to pull their war chariots, and known as the Celtic Pony. It has been claimed that the Exmoor descends from primitive ponies that survived the Ice Age in Alaska, crossed to Russia and then drifted southwards. Even less is known about the ancestry of the Exmoor's neighbor, the Dartmoor, and that of its near neighbor, the New Forest. Both, however, have occupied their current habitats for centuries; the mention of a "wild" pony in the Domesday Book of 1085 refers to one living in the area of the New Forest.

The Fells and Dales are believed to have been descended from the Celtic pony, but owe much of their sturdy makeup today to the Friesian horses brought over by the Romans.

Adapting for survival

All these ponies have adapted physically and in lifestyle to withstand the conditions in which they live. The Shetland ponies, for example, who perhaps have the coldest conditions to contend with, develop immensely thick coats in the winter with long, heavy manes and forelocks that fall way down their necks and right over their faces. They have a reputation for being able to fatten on almost anything, and they are a common sight at the water's edge in winter foraging for seaweed or scrounging the odd fish head from the local fishermen.

Winter conditions for the Exmoor are often far from cosy out on the bleak moors of Devon and they, too, develop a dense coat consisting of a fine, thick underlayer which acts like an insulating blanket, and an outer layer of longer, waterproofed hairs. Rain runs off without penetrating through and snow will sit on top of the ponies' backs, often taking a considerable time to melt. The ponies are forced to dig through the snow on the ground to find meager grazing underneath. In spring, they learn to avoid inviting patches of fresh green grass that are in fact the top-growths of treacherous boggy ground. These they shun until, dried by the winds, the rich grass can be grazed without fear or danger.

The Icelandic Pony is a tough little animal living in Iceland, many still seen roaming in semi-wild herds, although, like the ponies of Britain, they have in principle been domesticated for centuries. These ponies were originally taken to Iceland by Norse settlers in the late ninth and early tenth centuries, and once again the fact that they survived a sea crossing of some 600 miles in those days of erratic sea travel gives a strong indication of their toughness.

These ponies have adapted in their wild state to feed off the lichen-stems that hang from the trees, and, like the Shetland ponies, they have quite a taste for fish. In bad times, the ponies will even gnaw the wood on which fish has been dried. In spite of the fact that they live in semi-wild conditions, it is difficult to class these ponies as "wild" for they are the most friendly and docile of animals – although the early Norsemen gave vent to their bloodlust by engaging the friendly little ponies in savage horse fights.

Right: These elegant gray Camargue horses are typical of the herds which roam the marshy swamplands of the Rhône delta in France, surviving on the scrub growing in the area.

White horses

Throughout Europe, there are little groups of feral horses – usually offered some protection by man in terms of ownership, but for the main part roaming free – finding their own food and fending for themselves. In France, the beautiful white Camargue horses roam the marshy swamplands of the Rhône Delta and in Germany, in Westphalia, there is a herd of feral ponies called Dulmens that has inhabited its wooded reserve for some 600 years. In the wild interior of Sardinia – still the heart of bandit country – a race of wild horses lives among the cork trees, tangled briars and ferns. Very little is known of these horses for few people visit the region, and it is said that there is a secret place where the mares shelter to give birth and another where old horses go to die, but the location of neither is known. It is also uncertain whether any herds of ancient Przewalski's Horse or its relatives are still to be found living wild in far Eastern Europe or Central Asia. Generally it is thought that the only living specimens of these ancient breeds today are to be found in zoos.

Left: Dulmen ponies, which combine hardiness with an even temperament, come from Westphalia in Germany and have inhabited their wooded reserve for some 600 years.

Below: A semi-wild herd of Camargue ponies standing peacefully at Tour de Valat, a far cry from their dangerous life in the noise and blood of the bullrings.

Possibly the "wildest" of all wild horses in the modern world – in terms of temperament and the way in which they live – are the Brumbies of Australia. Like the United States of America, Australia has no indigenous horses; the Brumby is the descendant of animals taken to the continent during the Gold Rush of the mid-nineteenth century. With their minds focused only on the precious metal, prospectors had little time for their horses and often left them to wander off into the bush to a life of freedom.

Conditions here were as harsh as anywhere in the world, with the dry stony ground supporting very little in the way of fodder or water reserves. The Brumbies took to it with enthusiasm, however, and bred prolifically to produce a race of tough, wily scrub horses with a nature that is said to be so wild and intractable that if they are caught, they are almost impossible to train into safe domestic mounts.

Just why these animals have been called Brumbies is uncertain; explanations range from it being derived from the aboriginal word for wild *baroomby* or from a station in Queensland which was called Baramba, to a pioneer horse-breeder named James Brumby.

Below: In the Australian outback a cowhand rounds up Brumbies, possibly the wildest of all wild horses left, thought to be descended from horses imported during the Gold Rush.

What price survival?

A question mark hangs over the future of many of these feral horses, for their number has consistently and significantly diminished over recent decades.

So successfully did the descendants of the first horses taken to Australia adapt to the conditions of their wild habitat that they bred in huge numbers. In the early decades of the twentieth century, their numbers were swelled by horses who, no longer needed for the new mechanized agriculture, were turned out loose on the ranges. Before long the wild horses became a real menace to farmers, trampling and grazing pastures, tearing down fences and churning up precious water holes. As a result station hands in the outback found they had a new job – that of "Brumby-running". The idea was to capture the wild horses by running them into corals. This done, some were kept in the hope they could be trained and sold for saddle horses and the rest were simply shot. So successful was this "control" of the Brumbies that very few still exist in the wild outback today.

In Europe and Great Britain feral ponies fare much better, and in most places a benevolent overseeing eye is kept on them to ensure they are not endangered. Seen in some ways as an important part of a country's heritage, Protection Associations and Societies have been formed to check that, at a time when their habitat is being continually eroded by the onward path of civilization, they nevertheless survive.

These horses have not always been treated with such consideration, however. In Great Britain, the Dales ponies suffered considerably when mechanization began to replace them in traction and agriculture. With no work for them to do, the ponies became a liability to the farmers who owned the fells over which they wandered; grazing eaten by horses was grazing not available for money-earning sheep and cattle. Once more ponies were slaughtered on a huge scale, and there was a time earlier this century when the Dales pony came near to extinction. It was saved by

Left: The Andalusian, descended from the Spanish Barb, was the foremost horse in Europe until the eighteenth century. His great presence, valuable both in the show ring and the bullring, has had enormous influence on other European breeds, notably the beautiful white Lipizzaners.

Right: Lipizzaners, famous for their spectacular feats of dressage at the Spanish Riding School in Vienna, are born dark brown or black, becoming whiter with age. These were bred at the State Stud at Piber.

the birth of a new industry – tourism, which brought with it the idea of pony-trekking as a pleasant way to enjoy the beautiful scenery of the Dales' home. The pony's common sense, docility and knowledge of its homeland made it ideal for the job, and the breed was saved. Many now still wander the fells, watching their relatives carrying tourists on their broad backs.

The Exmoor Ponies had a bad time during World War II when many were slaughtered for meat. Those that escaped the butcher's knife, however, found that their home was used as a tank training ground and many of the ponies fell victim to the stray bullets of practicing soldiers. The breed as a whole suffered greatly from this time, and rebuilding the herds has been a painstaking business, accounting for the relatively small number of pure-bred Exmoor Ponies left today.

Saddest of all the stories of the decimation of wild herds is that of the proud Mustangs of the American plains. Vast herds of these animals were once a common sight in North America. At the turn of the century, there were estimated to be two million Mustangs on the prairies; by 1968 there were an estimated 17,000 and, three years later, just 10,000. Only man can be blamed for this. He took them to their slaughter in their thousands in the Boer War and World War I; he has killed them for chicken feed and fertilizer or because he wanted to graze his own livestock on the public land of their habitat. And they have been killed in order to preserve the land for big game that attracts wealthy hunters as well as for their hide and for their meat.

Protection has come to the Mustangs, but it did not do so until 1971 when a law was passed making it a federal offense to harass or kill a wild horse. Hopefully it came just in time to prevent the wild horse from becoming extinct in America for the second time.

The desert tribesmen bred their horses selectively for speed, stamina and soundness, qualities which many of their descendant breeds have inherited.

Although there is an enormous number of different breeds of horses, just three separate classifications are used to define the various types. There are "hot bloods", "cold bloods" and "warm bloods" – descriptions which are not of course related to body-temperature, but to origins.

Those horses called hot bloods are of Oriental or Eastern origin – the Arabian, Thoroughbred, Anglo-Arab and a few others – all highly-strung, courageous and fiery animals. Cold bloods are the big draught horses, the farm workers and load haulers, strong and docile heavyweights like the Shire and the Percheron. The warm bloods are the mixtures or crosses of hot and cold. Among them will be found show jumpers and other good competition horses (except racing, which uses hot bloods). By and large, these horses are less inclined to be difficult, although temperament will obviously vary, depending to some extent on quantity of hot and cold blood in the ancestry. Breeds such as the Standardbred and Quarter horse, the Oldenburg and the Selle Français are examples of warm bloods.

The term half-breed applies to a cross between a Thoroughbred and a native pony or heavy horse. If this half-bred is then mated to another Thoroughbred the progeny is a three-quarter-bred.

The Arabian

The origins of this beautiful horse are obscure, but it is thought that the Arab horse was established on the Arabian peninsula as early as 5000 BC. What is more certain is that the early Muslim invasions through the Iberian peninsula and up into France spread the Arabian blood into Europe. However, it is not only in Europe that this horse's influence has been felt; Marco Polo writing in about AD 1290 says: "It is from this port in Aden that the merchants obtain pure Arabian destriers (war horses) from which they make such great profits in India."

The Arabian horse would not have survived so successfully had it not been found to be superior in stamina, speed and prepotency wherever it has been introduced. The desert tribesmen bred their horses selectively for type, stamina, soundness, speed and strength over many generations. These characteristics have been faithfully passed on to the progeny, and because of this prepotency, the Arabian has been continually crossed with virtually all types of horses, to improve and refine future generations.

The Arabian has left his mark, too, on the British native ponies, particularly the Welsh Mountain pony, which reflects Arab ancestry in its finely shaped, pretty head. France has made extensive use of the Arab to produce the French Anglo-Arab horse as well as to influence the French Trotter. Hungary and Poland recruited the horse for most of their cavalry divisions from Arab crosses, while in Russia the Akhal-Teke and the Orlov Trotter – probably Russia's best known breeds – both have Arabian blood in their veins. In the USA, a country which has the distinction of having the largest population of pure-bred Arabians, the Morgan and the Standardbred reputedly can be traced back to Arabian parentage.

The essential appearance of all Arabian horses is similar, although those bred in different parts of the world tend to have a differing type, though still recognizable as Arab. The usual height is between 14.2 to 15.2 h.h. The head of the Arab is perhaps its most characteristically recognizable feature; it is refined and "dished" – slightly bulging just above, below and between the eyes so as to make the nose look concave – with large, bright eyes, flared nostrils and a small, tapering muzzle. The neck should appear well set on to the body; the back should be short and strong with the ribs well rounded, and the tail set perhaps a little higher than is general in most other breeds. The legs should be hard, clean and well-formed, and the action is characterized by an apparently almost "floating" movement, particularly at the trot.

Above: The Arabian, famous for its elegance, speed and spirit, is the fountainhead of the world's breeds and has had an enormous influence on many of them.

The Thoroughbred

The Thoroughbred must be counted as the most successful "invention" of the horse world. As interest grew to make racing a professional, as well as hugely popular, sport, faster and bigger horses were demanded, and it was found that the offspring of home-bred mares and Eastern sires produced horses with these qualities. In consequence, nearly 300 years ago, Eastern stallions were imported to Britain to be crossed with English mares of mixed pedigrees. The most famous of these stallions are known as the Byerley Turk, the Darley Arabian and the Godolphin Arabian, and between them they have produced a dynasty of great racehorses. The Byerley Turk, imported in 1689 by a Captain Robert Byerley who captured him from the Turks and subsequently rode him into battle, established the famous Herod line, which can be traced down through several highly successful stallions – among them, the Tetrarch.

The Darley Arabian was imported from Syria in 1704. He sired the famous Flying Childers, as a result of a mating with an Oriental mare called Betty Leedes. He was also the founder of the Eclipse line – Eclipse was one of the greatest Thoroughbreds of all time.

The Godolphin Arabian, third of the "founding fathers" (as these three Eastern stallions are known) was given to the King of France, who sold him to Lord Godolphin in England in 1730. His prime claim to fame was his grandson, Matchem, and subsequently the Matchem line.

Such was the influence of these stallions and others similar to them that their stock was exported all over the world. North America, France, Italy, Germany, Australia, New Zealand, South America and countries of the East were the principal importers and all then produced their own Thoroughbred horses.

Although bred originally for the racecourse, the Thoroughbred's influence has spread far and wide and has been responsible time and again for the upgrading and formation of other breeds and types. As mentioned earlier, judicious crossings of the Thoroughbred with native mares has produced many of the world's warm-bloods – among them the Selle Français, the German Trakehner and the American Standardbred. By crossing Thoroughbreds with Irish Draught or Cleveland Bays, top class hunters, show jumpers and eventers have been produced, and quality riding ponies are often the result of native pony and Thoroughbred crosses.

The Thoroughbred's most notable characteristic is perhaps his turn of speed, particularly over a short distance. He can be anything from 14.2 to 17 h.h. and any solid color, although bay, brown and chestnut predominate. His action should be free, with a long "ground-covering" stride. Good specimens are characterized by their excellent conformation – well laid back shoulders, elegant neck, short, strong body which is deep through the girth and has strong well-muscled quarters, and clean, hard legs with at least 8 inches (20 cm) of bone, measured round the top of the cannon bone below the knee. The head should give an instant impression of quality, refinement and intelligence and the overall appearance is one of proud bearing and great nobility.

Left: Derived from the Arabian, the Thoroughbred can lay claim to being the most beautiful horse in the world, and its speed and stamina make it a superb racehorse.

The Standardbred

A horse whose development is closely connected to that of the Thoroughbred is the Standardbred. In 1780, a Thoroughbred gray called Mambrino, who had raced successfully as a three-, four- and five-year-old, sired a horse called Messenger. Also a gray, Messenger's pedigree included crosses to all three founding fathers (see above). In 1788, this horse was exported to North America, where he stood at stud in Pennsylvania, New York and New Jersey. He was subsequently acknowledged as the foundation sire of the Standardbred, now the famous American trotting and pacing racehorse.

Bred for flat racing, Messenger had never been entered in trotting races, but by the 1840s his descendants were winning such races, then run under saddle. It was his progeny, Hambletonian, sired in 1849, who really put this line into the limelight as the producer of the world's greatest harness racehorse. Hambletonian's progeny triumphed again and again on the racecourse and four of his sons were destined to become the founders of the bloodlines to which virtually all American Standardbred trotters and pacers today can be traced.

The Standardbred stands 14 to 16 h.h. and is usually black, bay, brown or chestnut in color. Powerfully and robustly built, with a little less refinement than the Thoroughbred, he nevertheless possesses the thoroughbred's stamina and courage. As referred to above, Standardbreds either trot or pace, these gaits being largely inherited. The diagonally-gaited trotters are described as being "line-gaited" or "passing-gaited". In the former the opposite front and hind feet move in direct line with each other when viewed from in front or behind, while in the latter the hind feet are placed outside the front feet. Pacers move the hind and fore legs on the same side together.

The Saddlebred

Originally known as the Kentucky Saddler, after the state in which the breed evolved, the Saddlebred was developed during the early nineteenth century. Selective cross-breeding of the Thoroughbred, Morgan and Narragansett Pacer produced a horse with stamina, comfortable gaits and a pleasant temperament. The plantation owners in the deep south found this horse to be ideal either for riding over rough ground or for driving in harness.

Today the Saddlebred is bred mainly for the show ring where it is exhibited in three classes – the three-gaited, the five-gaited and in harness. The paces of three-gaited Saddlebreds are the walk, trot and canter, while the five-gaited horse also performs the "slow gait" and the "rack". The slow gait is a four-time, high stepping movement; the rack is similar but faster. It is officially described as "a flashy, fast four-beat gait free from any lateral motion or pacing".

Saddlebreds stand 15 to 16 h.h. and are usually bay, black, chestnut or gray in color. Intelligent, quiet and

Above: Closely connected to the Thoroughbred but with a little less refinement, the Standardbred is used for either trotting or pacing.

Below: The American Saddlebred used to be called the Kentucky Saddler. Today he is used in the showring in classes for three- and five-gaited horses.

gentle, they have a well-shaped head, arched neck and short back and well muscled quarters with the tail set high. In fact, this showy appearance of the tail is obtained by nicking the dock muscles and resetting the tail. The limbs should be straight, strong and muscular with long pasterns and the feet are allowed to grow long.

The Tennessee Walking Horse

This is another breed developed by the plantation owners as a general working animal. Like the Saddlebred, he has Narragansett Pacer, Morgan and Thoroughbred blood in his veins, as well as that of the Standardbred. The Tennessee Walking Horse is one of America's most popular breeds and it has been claimed that his peculiar four-beat gaits make him the most comfortable ride in the world.

These four-beat gaits are a flat walk and a running walk, both described as a "basic, four-cornered lick", that is a 1-2-3-4 beat with each foot hitting the ground separately at regular intervals. The flat walk should be "loose, bold and square" with plenty of shoulder motion. The running walk is also executed with the characteristic loose ease of movement, pulling with the fore feet, pushing and driving with the hind. The third gait, known as the ·"rocking-chair canter", is a high rocking motion, characterized by a smooth and collected movement.

In height, the Tennessee Walking Horse varies between 15 and 16 h.h. and his color is black or chestnut. Of good conformation with a somewhat plain head, strong arched neck, sloping shoulder and strong powerful body and quarters, he is noted for his equable temperament.

The Morgan

The Morgan is another horse with Thoroughbred ancestry, this time mixed with Arab and Welsh Cob. The breed's foundation sire, a stallion called Justin Morgan, is believed to have foaled in Massachusetts in about 1795, but the horse was given the name of his second owner, who came from Vermont. Standing only 14 h.h. this horse was found to be a very useful all-round work horse on the farm, excellent in harness and for hauling timber. He excelled in weight-pulling contests, in which he was rarely beaten. He was also a prepotent sire, passing on his qualities of toughness, versatility and courage.

Today, the Morgan is an ideal pleasure horse both under Western and English saddle, as well as in harness. Of good, stocky conformation, he stands between 14.1 and 15.2 h.h. and has a short back with good depth through the girth and muscular quarters. The neck is also well muscled, the head small and attractive and the legs short and strong. The color is usually bay, chestnut, black or brown.

Below: The American-bred Morgan is versatile and active and makes an ideal all-round pleasure horse.

Above: Appaloosas are agile and fast and often used for Western riding. This Appaloosa has a blanket spotted coat.

The Quarter Horse

The Quarter Horse was developed in Virginia and the Carolinas, based on Spanish mares crossed with English stallions imported around 300 years ago. This tough, compact little horse originally used to perform work in harness and under saddle. His extreme agility made him especially useful for herding cattle, so he found particular favor on the cattle ranches.

The Quarter Horse was also found to be extremely fast over short distances, and so became a popular mount for impromptu races regularly run on any convenient track or road. These sprints, traditionally staged over a quarter-mile, gave rise to the horse's name. When organized Thoroughbred racing took over in popularity from these contests, the Quarter Horse returned to cattle ranching and pleasure riding, excelling particularly in Western rodeos. Quarter Horse track racing has recently undergone something of a revival, however, and now many of these attractive little horses are to be seen on the racetrack.

In conformation, the Quarter Horse is strong, powerful and muscular with a short back, well-developed quarters, sloping shoulders and with good depth through the chest. The head should be relatively short and wide and the limbs short and clean with big flat knees and hocks. Overall, the horse is well-built with pleasing proportions and a kind disposition. Standing 14.3 to 16 h.h., he may be any solid color, although chestnuts are most popular. Such has been his popularity that the Quarter horse has been exported all over the world, particularly to Australia for work on the huge cattle stations.

The Appaloosa

Cave paintings dating back some 20,000 years depicting horses with spotted markings have been found throughout Europe. As was seen earlier, horses are believed to have returned to the American continent in the sixteenth century, when they were transported over by the Spanish conquistadores, and subsequently brought north from Mexico by the Plains Indians. One tribe, the Nez Percé Indians, inhabited the Palouse Valley in the northwest of America in a region bordering Oregon, Washington and Idaho. Here they selectively bred a tough, sure-footed horse with a spotted coat and great endurance, similar to the spotted horse known to have existed in other parts of the world, but identified today as the Appaloosa.

The Appaloosa coat pattern is distinctive and may be any of the following: leopard-spotted (dark spots on a white background); snowflake (light spots on a dark background); frost (white specks on a dark background); blanket (spots on the loins and quarters only) or marbelized (mottled all over the body). The mane and tail tend to be sparse and the small, neat hooves are striped vertically black-and-white. He stands 14.3 to 15.2 h.h., is very agile and fast and characterized by a tractable temperament.

The Appaloosa today is a popular parade horse because of the peculiar, but attractive markings, as well as being used for Western and leisure riding. The breed is produced worldwide.

Great Britain has a number of native breeds of ponies and horses. Representatives of the ponies are still to be found running free in their various regions (see Chapter 2), but there are also many studs devoted to their breeding.

The Welsh Breeds

Among the most popular are the Welsh breeds which are divided into four types: Welsh Mountain, Welsh Pony, Welsh Pony of Cob Type and the Welsh Cob. Reference was first made to these ponies in Roman times and evidence suggests that they have changed little since then. Thoroughbred and Arab blood have both been used in the later development of the Welsh Mountain pony but careful selection within the breed itself has ensured that, once considered established, the breed was free from outside influences.

During the nineteenth century, farmers started to raise the ponies on the Welsh hillsides along with their cattle. Found to be excellent mounts for children, the demand for them has grown steadily ever since. Many have been exported, particularly to the USA, where they are now bred extensively.

Regarded by many as being the most beautiful and intelligent of the native breeds, the Welsh Mountain pony is hardy and spirited. Standing up to 12 h.h. he may be any whole color, but is probably most usually thought of as gray. His head should be small and clean-cut with big bold eyes and small ears. The neck should be of good length with the shoulder well laid back, the back and loins muscular and strong and with good depth through the girth. There should be plenty of good dense bone and the action should be free, quick and straight from the shoulder.

The Welsh Pony is a slightly larger version of the Welsh Mountain, standing up to 13.2 h.h. For many generations he was the traditional mount of the shepherds on the hills of Wales, but now his main use too is as a child's riding pony, having the same good temperament, bone, substance and hardiness as the Welsh Mountain pony.

The Welsh Pony of Cob Type is the stronger counterpart of the Welsh Pony with, as the name suggests, the addition of Cob blood. At the beginning of this century there were several good sires of this breed, but after World War II the numbers were seriously diminished. However, now the breed's popularity has increased again and, like the other Welsh breeds, these ponies have been exported round the world. They make an ideal family pony, standing up to 13.2 h.h.; they are active, sure-footed and strong and have proved to be good jumpers, as well as good harness ponies.

The Welsh Cob was established as a breed during the twelfth century, and by the fifteenth century was being used extensively as an all-round work horse on the farm as well as for personal transport. Today he is a perfect family horse, standing over 13.2 h.h. and being strong, hardy, intelligent, kind and willing. He makes a good jumper and is excellent in harness, giving him the high flown reputation in some circles as "the best ride and drive animal in the world".

Left: Britain has nine breeds of native pony, many of which still run wild in their natural habitat. They are generally hardy breeds and make ideal children's ponies.

The Shetland

The Shetland Islands at the northern tip of Scotland are the home of the smallest of the British native breeds, the Shetland pony. The origins of this diminutive breed are uncertain, but the isolation of his homeland has ensured no infusions of outside blood. His small size (average 40 inches/1 meter) once made him much in demand for work in coal mines, but on his home islands he was used for transport and general work on the crofts. The Shetland is thick set, deep and broad in build with short legs and a short, sturdy back. He has a profuse mane and tail and can be any color.

The Highland

The Highland is another Scottish pony used for general farm work, work on the deer moors, and, more recently, as a trekking pony. He is very versatile, makes a good family pony and has been found to be a good foundation stock for breeding hunters and eventers. Not above 14.2 h.h., the Highland is strong and compact, deep-chested and with powerful quarters. Colors are usually dun, gray, brown and black.

Below: The smallest of the British Mountain and Moorland ponies is the Shetland, which were once used as pit ponies in the coal mines, because of their diminutive size.

The Dales and Fell

The Dales and Fell, found in the north of England, have similarities to each other in conformation and appearance, both having been influenced by the Friesian (see page 45). Both were once used as pack ponies to carry lead from the mines in the north of England, and as all-round work animals on the hill farms. Hardy and sure-footed, the Dales is still often seen in harness or as a trekking pony, and is ideally suited to either occupation. Usually black and standing no more than 14.2 h.h., the Dales is strong and powerful yet compact and well developed, and has fine silky hair at the heel. The Fell is a little smaller, averaging 13.2 h.h., and makes a good riding pony.

The Exmoor

The Exmoor is generally thought to be the oldest of the British native breeds and, together with the Dartmoor, comes from the southwest of England. His stamina, sure-footedness and strength brought him popularity in the 1920s and 1930s, particularly as a riding pony for both children and small adults. The breed's main characteristics are the brown, bay or dun-colored rather harsh coat with its mealy-colored markings around the eyes, muzzle and flanks, the thick tail that is "fan-like" at the top and the "toad" eyes, so-called because they are wide-set, large and prominent. Maximum height is 12.3 h.h.

Left: The Exmoor is the oldest and one of the best-loved of the British native breeds.

Above: Quality ponies like this Dartmoor prizewinner have dominated British show rings for years.

Right: This New Forest foal has had infusions of most of the native British breeds over preceding generations.

The Dartmoor

The Exmoor's neighbor, the Dartmoor, was used in the tin mines of the southwest of England 1000 years ago. Today his popularity as a children's riding pony is surpassed by few other breeds. Standing no more than 12.2 h.h., the Dartmoor is kind, quiet, gentle and reliable. If crossed with a Thoroughbred, a larger pony naturally results, but one that, while it is active and possessed of speed and stamina, nevertheless keeps the inherent pony characteristics and temperament of the Dartmoor.

The New Forest

The New Forest pony has had infusions of most of the other native breeds over the years, plus Arab and Thoroughbred. It is, therefore, not easy to ascribe to him specific characteristics and a definite type. However, by and large the New Forest ponies are versatile and willing, with a good temperament. These characteristics and their size, 12.2 to 14.2 h.h., make them useful family ponies.

The Connemara

The Connemara comes from the west coast of Ireland, where he has long been used for general work around the farm. Versatile, sturdy, strong and hardy, the Connemara makes an ideal family pony; at 13 to 14.2 h.h., he is small enough for a child, yet quite strong enough to carry an adult. His intelligence, tractable temperament and agility make him suitable for all riding pursuits.

The Shire

In contrast to the British pony breeds so far discussed, the Shire is one of the largest horses in the world. So named because it originated in the "shires" (counties) of England, it is a descendant of the great horses used in medieval times to carry armored knights into battle. Up to 18 h.h., the Shire is immensely strong with a relatively fine head, and a lot of feather on his long legs. He was used extensively in agriculture until mechanization took over, at which time there was a noticeable decline in the numbers of the breed. However, there has recently been a revival of interest in these, and other, heavy horses, resulting in the Shire being used again on the land in some areas, as well as finding favor as a dray horse.

The Suffolk

The Suffolk, a native of the East Anglian region of England, can be traced back to the early sixteenth century and was bred to work on the land. He is the only clean-legged British draught horse (one with no feather round the fetlocks), making him specially suitable for work in heavy soils. Standing 16 to 16.2 h.h. the Suffolk is always chestnut in color and may still be seen working the land in some areas.

The Clydesdale

The heavy Clydesdale originates from Scotland, where local mares were crossed with Flemish stallions during the eighteenth century to produce a horse with greater weight and substance. Standing about 16.2 h.h. and also used for agricultural work, the Clydesdale has a profusion of feather on the heel. A very active horse, he is usually bay, brown or gray, and has a lot of white on him, mainly on the legs and face, often extending into the body.

Below: The versatile Connemara comes from the West of Ireland. This breed is believed to have existed since the sixth century.

Right: The Shire's ancestors were the "great horses" of medieval times – now they are often used as dray horses.

The Selle Français

The Selle Français or French Saddle Horse is a "quality" horse (i.e. of good conformation and appearance) of 15.2 to 16.3 h.h., usually chestnut in color. The breed was developed when the English Thoroughbred was first exported to France and crossed with local French mares towards the end of the eighteenth century. In the Normandy region a fast trotting horse was also developing from the progeny of Thoroughbred stallions and Norman mares and became known as the French Trotter. The Selle Français had French Trotter blood introduced to produce horses of stamina, quality and jumping ability as well as good conformation and temperament. Today, the breed is used extensively in Europe for eventing and show jumping.

The Camargue

The "white horse of the sea", the Camargue pony, is native to the swampland around the Rhône delta of southern France. A hardy pony, standing up to 14.2 h.h., he survives on the rough grass and salt water of the region. Although small, he is sturdy and robust and provides an excellent mount for the "guardians", the men who herd the cattle of the area. Camargue ponies are used by these men, too, when they show off their expertise by working the black bulls, also indigenous to the Camargue region, in the bullring.

Above: This Selle Français is pictured at Haras du Pin, the French National Stud.

Below: Camargue horses provide excellent mounts for herdsmen or for the "guardians".

Continental Heavy Breeds

The Percheron from the Perche region of France is often considered to be a more sensitive horse than other heavy breeds, perhaps because of his Arab ancestry. Standing 15.2 to 17 h.h. he is usually gray or black and combines grace with power.

From Brittany comes the Breton of which there are three distinct types: the Draught Breton, developed from infusions of Ardennais, Percheron and Boulonnais blood, the Postier based on Hackney and Norfolk Roadster blood and the now rare Corlay. Standing between 15 to 16 h.h., the Breton is usually roan, chestnut or bay and makes an active work horse.

The French Ardennais and the Belgian Ardennes, heavy breeds from these respective countries, are very similar in appearance and build. Both are around 15.3 h.h., bay, roan or chestnut in color, stocky, compact and heavily built, and with a willing temperament which makes them ideal for all draught work. Both had infusions of Brabant blood (a heavy horse from Belgium which has been used to sire a number of heavy breeds). Another close relation is the Dutch Draught developed from Brabant and Belgian Ardennes blood. Standing up to 16.3 h.h., he is massively built and usually chestnut, bay or gray.

Below: The Belgian Ardennes is stocky and compact and makes a willing draught horse.

Right: With Arab ancestry, the Percheron is more highly-strung than other heavies.

The Hanoverian

The principal German warm blood, the Hanoverian, is of mixed Holstein ancestry (see below). Great Britain's German-born George II founded a stud at Celle in northern Germany in 1735 to produce a strong, all-purpose horse with sufficient quality to perform under saddle and powerful enough to work on the land. Today, made more elegant and lighter by Thoroughbred and Trakehner blood, the breed is in demand for show jumping and dressage, and, as a 16 to 17 h.h. strong, active horse, he is well able to fulfil this need.

Holstein

The Holstein from which the Hanoverian derived is a heavier type of riding horse of Andalusian origin which can be traced back to around the fourteenth century. Since that time, however, Eastern and later Thoroughbred blood was introduced to add quality and lightness to the breed, and today he is a useful general purpose horse possessing intelligence and a pleasant temperament. Powerfully built, with plenty of bone and substance and a deep body on short legs, he is in some demand today as a show jumper, eventer and dressage horse. This is a breed that is not, however, as popular as it used to be.

The Trakehner

The Trakehner, or East Prussian, a real "quality" horse, has much of the Thoroughbred about him. Years ago he was used as a coach horse and also extensively by the cavalry. He has plenty of speed, stamina and elegance and today he is used as a general riding horse and show jumper. Standing 16 to 16.2 h.h., the Trakehner has good conformation, an equable temperament, and may be any solid color. Halla, among the best known Trakehner of modern times, took German rider Hans Winkler to the World Championship show jumping title in 1955.

The Oldenburg

The Oldenburg is the heaviest of the German warm bloods and can be traced back to the seventeenth century. Based on the Friesian (see page 45), he was developed as a carriage horse and has had infusions of Eastern, Thoroughbred and Hanoverian blood. Later, more Thoroughbred was added to produce a lighter saddle horse, although the knee action peculiar to the carriage horse remains. Standing 16.2 to 17 h.h., he is usually brown, black or bay.

Left: The Hanoverian, originally used as a work horse as well as for riding, is the principal German warmblood and popular as a show jumper or for dressage.

Above: The distinctively colored Haflinger pony from the Austrian Tyrol is a tough and willing worker and is often used to give sleigh rides to tourists in winter.

The Haflinger

The Haflinger comes from the Austrian Tyrol, where he has been bred for hundreds of years out of heavy cold-blooded mares. All today's Haflingers can be traced back to the Arab stallion, El Bedavi. This in-breeding has resulted in a very similar appearance throughout the breed – a chestnut color with a flaxen mane and tail. Standing 13.3 to 14.2 h.h. the Haflinger is very strong, sure-footed, tough and a willing worker. His equable temperament makes him popular for agriculture and as a riding and pack pony.

All of those bred in Austria are branded with the letter "H" surrounded by an Edelweiss flower. Visitors to the Alpine regions will see them, often in pairs, drawing old-fashioned carriages full of delighted vacationers.

The Friesian

One of Europe's oldest breeds, the Friesian, comes from Holland, where he has existed since around 1000 BC. He was used as a weight-carrier and for agricultural work until trotting races became popular, for this was a sport at which he excelled. Oldenburg blood was then introduced, and today the breed flourishes as an all-round work horse used both for riding and driving. Standing 15 h.h., the Friesian is strong, compact and willing, with a fine head and short legs with feathered heels. The color is black.

The Gelderland

The popular Gelderland can be traced back to the last century when an old breed of native mares was crossed with Thoroughbreds, Holsteins and Arabian stallions. With later additions of Friesian and Oldenburg blood, the result is a strong, active horse of around 15.2 h.h. used today both as a carriage horse and saddle horse.

The Andalusian

Spain's Andalusian and Portugal's Lusitano are very similar in appearance, both old breeds containing Oriental blood. The Andalusian was the foremost horse in Europe until the eighteenth century. He possesses enormous presence. Great stress has always been laid on the purity of the blood lines and both breeds are intelligent, active, strong and courageous with thick wavy manes and tails. They stand approximately 15.2 h.h. and are usually white, gray or bay. The Lusitano is prized today for the bullring, the mounted horsemen – rejoneadores – needing highly-schooled horses on which to display their art.

The Andalusian was the foundation stock of the famous Lipizzaner, the beautiful horses used by the Spanish Riding School of Vienna. The horses were originally bred at Lipizza which was then part of the Austrian Empire (now in Yugoslavia).

Left: The popular Gelderland is a strong, active horse used both as a carriage horse and under saddle. Its breeding can be traced back to native mares in the last century.

Right: The Andalusian is an old breed containing Oriental blood and was the foundation stock of the Lipizzaners used at the Spanish Riding School of Vienna.

The Swedish Warm Blood

Of the Scandinavian breeds, the Swedish Warm Blood is the quality riding horse and his ancestry can be traced back some 300 years. Originally of mixed pedigree from horses imported from England, Denmark, France, Germany, Hungary, Russia, Spain and Turkey, the breed now has the reputation of producing excellent all-round horses with good conformation and temperament. Sound, strong, deep through the girth and with plenty of bone, the Swedish Warm Blood stands approximately 16.2 h.h. and is usually up to a fair weight. He has proved especially good as a dressage horse and has been exported worldwide.

The Norwegian Fjord

The best known of the Scandinavian ponies is the Norwegian Fjord which has inhabited Norway for thousands of years. The Vikings are known to have bred – or at least ridden – these ponies, and now they can be found all over Scandinavia, where they are used as pack ponies, farm workers and for riding and driving. Hardy and sure footed, with short, compact and muscular bodies, they are particularly useful in mountainous areas. Standing 13 to 14 h.h., their most distinctive characteristics are their straight-cut, erect, crescent-shaped mane and their dun coat color.

The Icelandic

Introduced into Iceland from Scandinavia, the Icelandic pony was used for centuries on the island to provide virtually the only means of transportation, particularly during the winter months. Extremely tough, agile, docile and intelligent, this pony is small and stocky, deep through the girth and with an abundance of mane and tail hair as well as feather at the heel. Owing to the island's isolation no outside blood has been introduced to the breed, which stands 12 to 13 h.h., and is used today for riding and in harness. He has five gaits, two distinct ones in addition to the walk, trot and canter. These are the "pace", which is a lateral gait, used to cover short distances at high speed, and the "tolt" which is a sort of running walk, used particularly when covering broken ground.

Below: The Norwegian Fjord pony has inhabited Norway for thousands of years and was used by the Vikings. Hardy and sure-footed, they are useful in mountainous areas.

Right: Tough, agile, docile and intelligent, the Icelandic pony was once virtually the only means of transport on the island. Little outside blood has been added to the breed.

The Orlov Trotter

The Orlov Trotter is one of the oldest Russian breeds dating back to the eighteenth century. He has a lot of Arab, Danish and Dutch blood and was bred for trotting races but, being strong and powerful with plenty of bone, he has also been popular as a carriage horse. He stands about 16 h.h. and is usually gray.

Other Breeds

Horses in the USSR are still bred for agricultural work and transportation, and in Eastern regions large herds are kept for meat and milk.

The Karabair, which belongs to the ancient breeds of central Asia, is only one of the horses bred in herds on the mountain foothills as a dual purpose riding and harness horse. The Mergel is bred in the Georgian republic for the same purpose, and the Bashkir from the Urals is bred for milk as well as agricultural work.

To develop a good competition animal, horses such as the Ukrainian and Latvian Riding Horse are being produced by crossing local mares with Thoroughbred, Arab or Hanoverian stallions. The results are strong horses with equable temperaments which are in demand for show jumping and dressage. The Budenny, originally used for cavalry purposes, is now also in demand for dressage, show jumping and racing after having had infusions of Thoroughbred blood. The Don, originally associated with the Cossacks, the famous horsemen from southern Russia, was bred as an army remount and has had infusions of Thoroughbred blood. The Akhal-Teke, of Arabian and Persian extraction, was also used in military campaigns, a hardy horse of great stamina now used principally for show jumping, dressage, and endurance riding.

Right: The Orlov Trotter is one of the oldest Russian breeds, dating back to the eighteenth century, and combines Arab, Danish and Dutch blood.

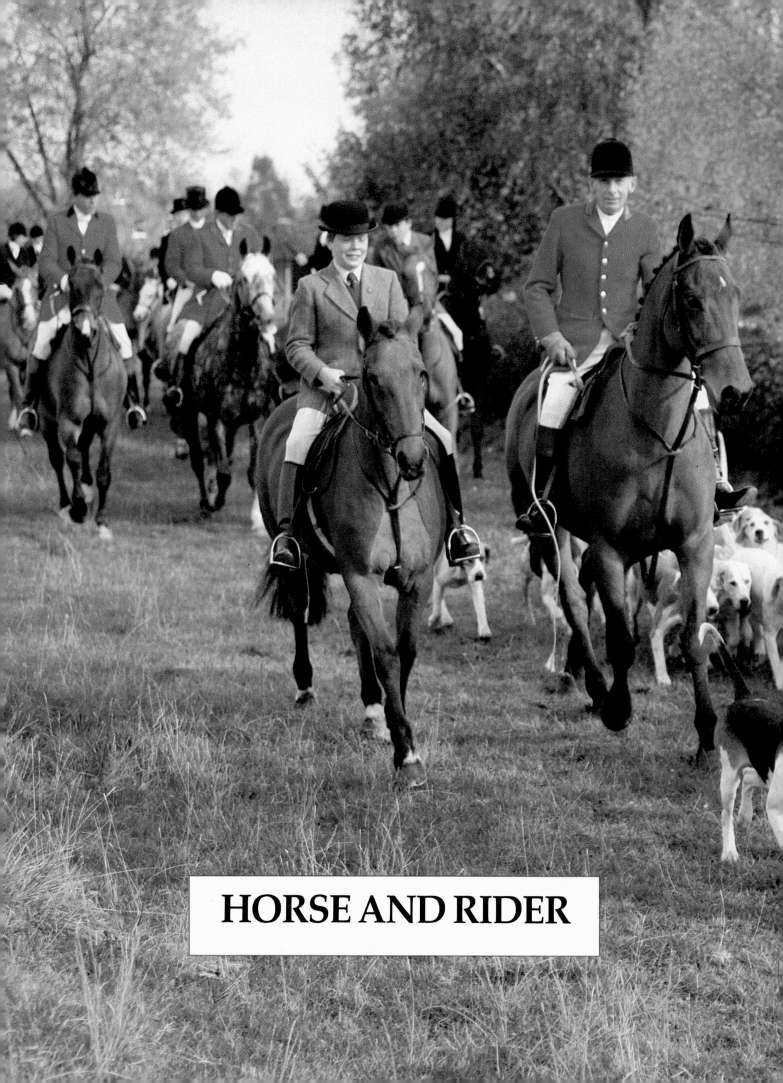

HORSE AND RIDER

A good temperament is extremely important when choosing a horse or pony. Here is a calm, friendly and willing pony of suitable size for a young rider.

Having learned to ride and thus experienced its joys, most people dream of having their own horse or pony. This dream quickly stretches to wild imaginings not just of happy rides along trails, but of repeated and unrivaled success in the competitive equestrian world. Before getting carried away, however, it is imperative to consider the business of horse-buying and owning both thoroughly and objectively. What sort of riding is it that you most want to do? Is show-jumping, eventing or the show ring to be a speciality, or is the requirement really just for a safe reliable animal for enjoyable leisure riding?

Answers to these questions will to a large degree be governed by your own riding ability, your stature and temperament, the facilities and time you have available for the general care and well-being of your horse – and the price you can afford to pay for him.

Riding ability

Novice riders usually tend to overrate their own abilities and expertise, with the result that they can end up buying a horse that is too much of a handful. At best this leads to a loss of confidence and at worst broken bones for the rider, while the horse will be confused, unhappy, and quite possibly ruined.

Buying a pony for a child presents similar problems.

It is all too easy to imagine that a child is more capable than he or she really is. Nor does it necessarily follow that an expensive, high-class pony will go straight to the top in competitive events just because the "pony always won with its previous rider". If the pony is beyond the child's capability to manage, it is more likely to put the young "hopeful" against riding for life. A calm, friendly and willing pony that a child can enjoy looking after and riding for pleasure is by far the most suitable starting point.

If the riding experience of the prospective buyer is limited to weekly rides at a local center, where quite possibly the horses have already had several hours' work that day, then to buy a highly-strung Thoroughbred could be disastrous. A half-bred animal with a more sedate outlook on life, one that would require neither the horsemanship nor the lavish care and attention a Thoroughbred would demand, would be infinitely more suitable. If, in addition, the available facilities amount to no more than a patch of pasture and a shelter rather than a stable and yard, a native pony or cross-bred will thrive where the highly-bred horse might suffer. A more highly-bred horse would be better suited to a competent and perhaps competitively-minded owner who, having already experienced the delights and drawbacks of horse-ownership, wants to go a stage or so further.

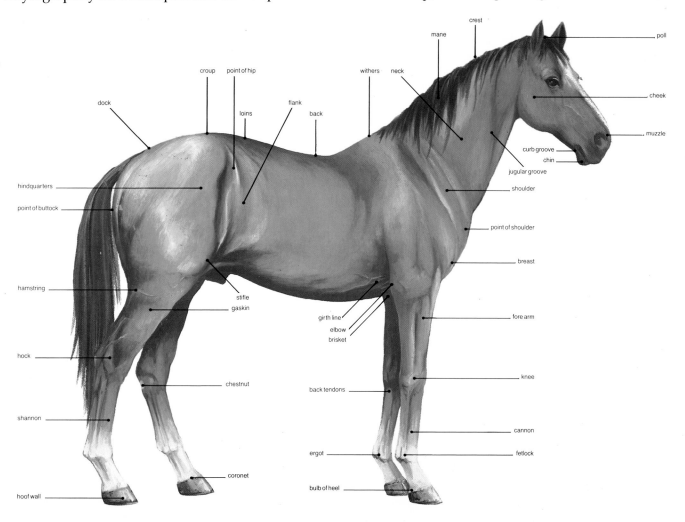

As far as personal stature and temperament are concerned, a rider with short legs is obviously best suited to a smaller, narrower horse. This facilitates not just riding, but also grooming, saddling-up, mounting and dismounting. Many people feel that smaller horses are frequently better balanced, cleverer, and have a stronger sense of self-preservation than larger animals – but be prepared for disagreement on these points from those who favor bigger breeds of horses.

If, on the other hand, the rider is tall and heavy with long legs, then a larger animal is obviously required. Bear in mind though, that the height of the horse does not bear directly on the weight he can carry. This is dependent more upon the amount of "bone" he has, and its density. An experienced horseman will be able to tell at a glance whether or not a particular horse is up to a prospective rider's weight – and this leads to another very important point when buying a horse. If, as the buyer, you are not experienced in the world of horses, always take somebody who does have that experience with you when you go to view a horse. An experienced person will be able to spot many of the pitfalls that a novice would never notice.

People with a somewhat volatile temperament can have an electrifying effect on a horse, while a calmer rider will send the same horse almost to sleep. It is sensible, therefore, for the more placid rider to acquire a horse with an "outward-going" character while a calmer horse is better suited to a more energetic rider. There is so much more enjoyment to be gained from a horse who is suited in make, shape, temperament and ability to that of his owner than one that is incompatible in these respects. It is worthwhile, therefore, giving this the highest consideration.

Livery

If time and facilities available to a rider are minimal, a horse may be kept at livery. Many people feel this inevitably takes a lot of fun out of owning a horse; certainly horse and owner do not have the same opportunities to get to know each other. It can also be extremely expensive in town and urban areas. However, if an animal is kept at full livery, then his all-round general care is placed in the hands of an expert – providing of course the establishment has been chosen with due care – while the owner should be able to ride him whenever he chooses.

Some livery establishments offer a system of part-livery, which is a cheaper alternative to full livery. Generally, the establishment still undertakes the full care of the horse, but it also uses him as a mount for other clients. As an owner in this situation, you should make sure you are happy about the ability of those riding your horse, and also that the animal is available for you at those times when you are free to ride.

Before you buy

When considering the price you can afford to pay for a horse do not forget to take into account the costs of feeding, shoeing, veterinarian's fees, insurance, saddlery repairs and the costs of traveling to shows and entry fees if you wish to compete, and then plan your budget accordingly.

Do not make the mistake of buying a very young animal because it is cheap, in the hope that the two of you can "learn together". You cannot and will not. A two- or three-year-old horse or pony may be cheap but at this age it will, or should, be unbroken; it will be immature, weak, and basically too young to be ridden until it is four years old. Unless you are a very competent rider or have access to constant professional help it is inadvisable to buy anything under six years old and, really, the best age to acquire a ready-made horse is between about six and ten years of age. The price gets higher up to about the age of seven, and decreases slowly up to about the age of twelve, when it tends to drop more rapidly. Do not, however, discount a horse which is more than twelve years old; there are many extremely good horses over this age with a number of years' work still in them. To the novice rider in particular, they can give a lot of pleasure and confidence.

It is said that a good horse is never a bad color, but it is perhaps worth remembering, particularly if you have limited time to look after the animal, that grays are regarded as "rich men's horses" because of the time and work involved in keeping them clean and free from mud and stable stains. Remember, too, that geldings are probably easier to cope with overall, as mares can be a bit touchy and temperamental when they come into season. However, mares can, of course, be used for breeding at a later stage and this may be an important consideration to you.

Where to buy

Having decided on the kind of horse that would be suitable, together with where and how it is to be kept, there are several ways to go about buying it.

A reputable riding establishment may well find a client a suitable horse, especially if the animal is to be kept at livery there. Beware, however, of buying a favorite school horse, one who may be very quiet when ridden out, for remember he may well have had a few hours' work by then. Taken out of his familiar environment and living on his own, with less regular work, the same horse could well be more of a handful than is comfortable.

Regular visits to local shows or membership in a local riding club or pony club are often a good way to hear of horses and ponies that are coming up for sale. The important thing, however, is to discover *why* they are coming up for sale; it should be for a genuine reason – in the case of a pony, perhaps it has been outgrown by its present rider, for example. It is an advantage, too, to have seen the animal in action, particularly if you are able to judge its rider's expertise.

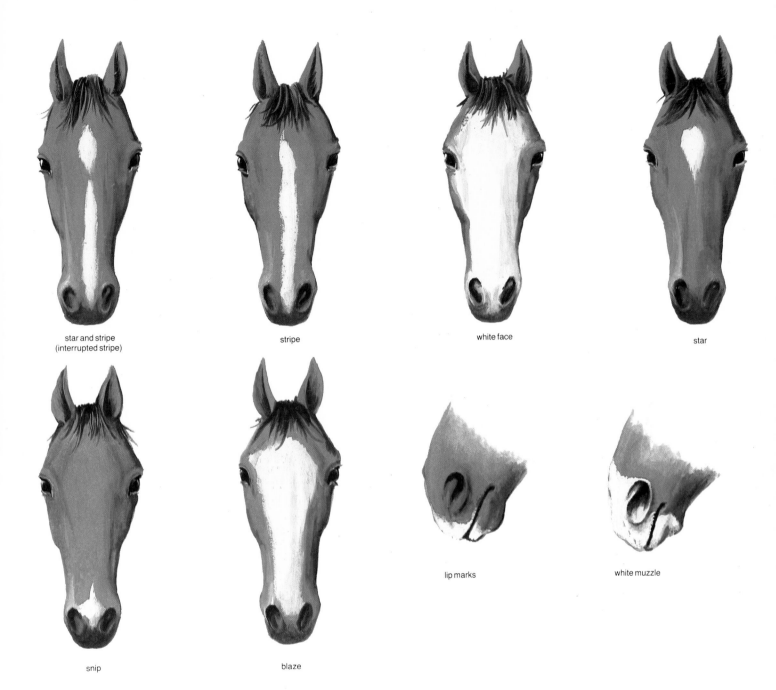

star and stripe
(interrupted stripe)

stripe

white face

star

snip

blaze

lip marks

white muzzle

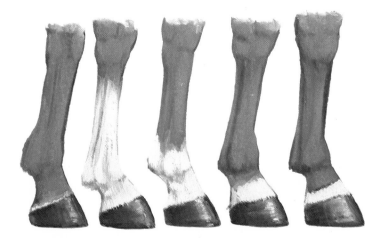

One of the easiest ways of identifying a horse is by its facial and leg markings. The facial marks shown here are among the commonest found. Terminology used to describe leg markings includes the *stocking* – which extends to the knee, *sock* – covering the fetlock and cannon, and *coronet* – the thin area just above the hoof.

Private sales are probably most frequently made through advertisements in the local paper and equestrian magazines. Look first at horses being advertised in your own area, partly because of the expense of traveling but mainly for the reason that owners are less likely to sell a bad horse to someone living in their neighborhood. You can often discover as much about the animal by reading between the lines to see what is not said as by what has actually been stated. For example, "interesting ride" probably implies that the animal is not suitable for a novice.

There are, of course, many reputable dealers who will be only too pleased to help you find just the right animal. Again, do not pretend that you are more experienced than you really are, for the dealer will be acting in good faith to sell you what he genuinely believes you want. A further possibility is to buy a horse at a recognized and reputable sale, but only the experienced should bid, not least because you will not be able to try out the animal before buying.

Assessing the horse

Having found a possible purchase, go to see it, taking an experienced and knowledgeable person with you. Look at the horse in his stable to gain an idea of the sort of "social" manners he has. Is he calm and friendly? Or does he try to barge out of the stable as soon as the door is opened? Does he rock continually from one forefoot to the other, or does he bite at the edge of the door or the manger, sucking in air as he does so. Both are stable vices known as weaving and crib-biting respectively, and both are detrimental to a horse's well-being and almost impossible to cure.

If a horse is first viewed out at pasture, note whether he is easy to catch, coming readily to the owner without the enticement of a bucket of feed. There is nothing more exasperating than trying to catch a horse who runs circles around you or moves away whenever he is approached.

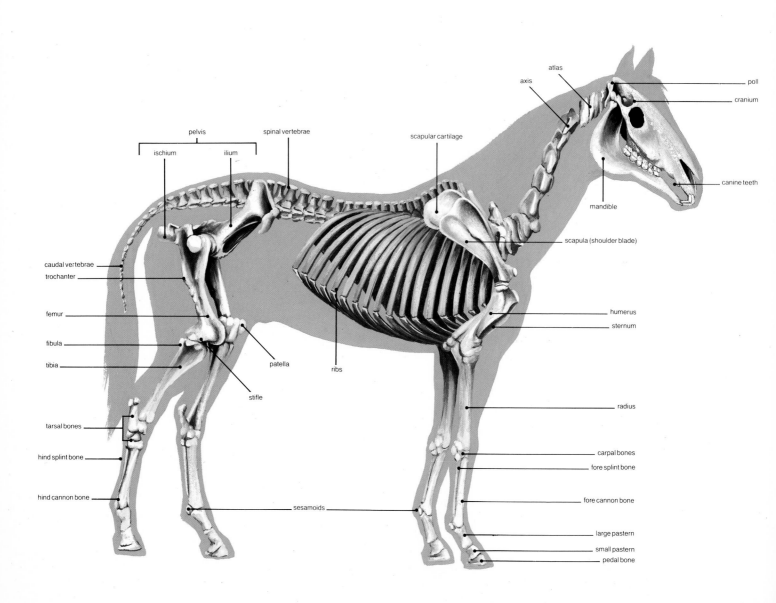

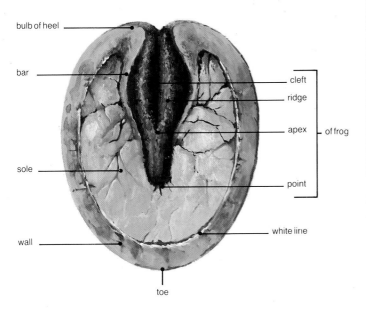

bulb of heel

bar

cleft

ridge

apex — of frog

sole

point

white iine

wall

toe

Conformation

Phrases such as "long back" "sloping shoulder", "deep through the girth" are used to denote faults and virtues. It is obviously not possible to give measurements here or indeed to define precisely what "round and muscled" quarters look like. All these terms are comparative, and become more meaningful when they are seen through the eyes of experience. This is why it is so important to be accompanied by someone with experience if you do not yet have it yourself.

Stand back and take a good look at the animal to assess his general conformation. Good conformation can best be described as "a near perfection of the overall make and shape as a result of a corresponding perfection in the component parts, where no one feature disturbs the overall symmetry". To help you a little further, perhaps the conformation required for a riding horse could be said to come somewhere between the polarized examples of the conformation required for the racehorse's speed (narrow and slender in build with a sloping shoulder allowing for a long, low stride) and the heavy horse's pulling power (short, thick bones, wide long body and upright shoulder for short strides).

It is logical that a horse of good overall proportions will have a longer active working life than one of poor conformation. Any deficiency is, after all, always a potential weakness. Action, good or bad, is the direct result of the corresponding conformation; straight, well-formed limbs producing a free straight movement with the horse properly balanced.

First look at his head. A well-bred horse will have a finely-shaped head, while a less well-bred one will be coarser and heavier, probably with a slight Roman (convex) nose. Large eyes, placed well to the front, wide nostrils and mobile ears, most often pricked forward, are all desirable qualities and indicate a generally good character and temperament. The head must be in proportion to the neck; a big heavy head on a long neck will cause too much weight to be carried on the forehand, resulting in the horse leaning on the rider's hands.

The neck should be streamlined into the shoulder in a graceful curve and the withers should be well defined (rather than "disappearing" into the back) if fitting of a saddle is not to be a difficulty. Low, flat withers tend to be accompanied by upright shoulders which produce a short stride and an uncomfortable ride as well as causing concussion to the legs. Conversely, high withers tend to accompany a good sloping shoulder which produces a long low stride and a comfortable ride.

The shoulder blades should be long in the riding horse with the elbow placed well clear of the ribs and well forward, thus lengthening the stride and producing a long, low action while reducing concussive wear-and-tear on the legs. The chest should be medium width and look in proportion to the neck and forelegs when viewed from the front, the forearm muscled and strong, the fetlocks and knees big and flat and the cannon bones short and straight. Pasterns should be of medium length – too short or too long are both potential weaknesses.

None of the leg joints should be puffy, as this denotes that the horse has already been worked hard and has suffered accordingly. The cannon bones should feel hard and cool, again with no tendency to puffiness.

The horse's body should be deep through the girth as this allows for expansion of the lungs. The back should be well-muscled and rise slightly to the croup; if it is too broad, there will be a tendency to a rolling action. It should not be dipped either, this being an indication of age, or too long or short. The latter will produce an uncomfortably bumpy ride, as well as limiting the engagement of the hindlegs and thereby the animal's speed.

There should be no hollow between the last rib and the hip bone; this indicates that it will be difficult to keep a horse in condition. Similarly, the loins should be short, muscular and powerful, and not slack.

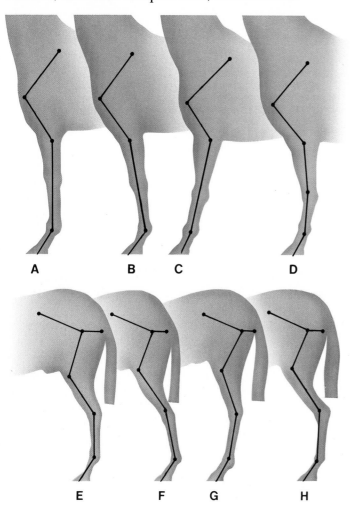

A First-rate. The hoof is seen at a point midway between the shoulder and elbow.
B Less stable. Positioning of hoof is off-center.
C Hoof too far forward. This is likely to result in tendon strain.
D Hollow kneed. This stance is likely to damage the knee ligaments.
E First-rate. The hoof is at a point midway between the stifle and buttock point.
F Less stable. The leg is too far back.
G The angle of the leg can result in injury.
H This conformation can strain the tendons of the fetlock.

Conformation – points to look out for:

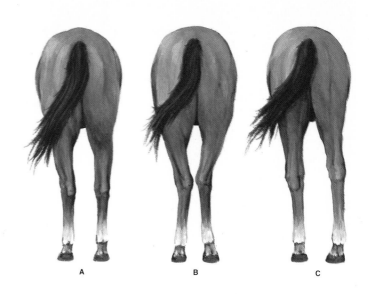

A shows the hindquarters of a horse with a good stance; B a cow-hocked stance; and C a bowlegged stance. B looks uncomfortable, but does not put as much strain on bones and tendons as C.

The croup, the highest point of the hindquarters, should be in a line with the withers; however, a very high croup can often be a sign of a good jumper, and is therefore sometimes called a "jumper's bump". The quarters should be round and muscled, and the hocks carried in a straight line from the point of the buttock to the ground. Hocks should not be overbent and curved on the front surface (sickle hocks) or carried well to the rear as the joint is then predisposed to damage as a result of uneven strain.

The feet should match one another in size and shape and point directly to the front; if one is "out-of-true" this denotes possible – or at least potential – lameness. Pick up the feet and note whether the heels are open and the soles slightly concave, as they should be. Horses with dropped soles are to be avoided, as are those with feet that look disproportionally small. Those with cracks or broken horn should be treated with suspicion, for the horse might well have recurring problems with his feet.

Trying the horse

Having studied the horse to check these points as far as you can, the next step is to ask for him to be led out in hand. Have him walked away from you in a straight line and then trotted back towards you. This will enable you to see if he moves with a straight action, or whether he throws a leg out, or crosses one forefoot over the other. Does he move "too close", so that he knocks one fetlock against the other? When you have seen his action, watch the owner saddle and bridle him and ask him to ride the horse for you so that you may see how he behaves.

When you first ride the horse, walk him for a while to get the feel of him before asking for a trot and canter on both reins. You will soon discover whether he is

one-sided or goes equally well on both reins, and then put him over a small fence. Ride him out of the yard and down the road a short way to discover whether he "naps" on leaving home and his reaction to traffic. Then take him back to his stable and remove the tack, observing how he reacts – whether he is nervous about his head as the bridle is removed for example.

Now and only now is the time to decide if you like the horse. However wonderful he appears, you must genuinely believe the two of you can get along together. If you do like him, ask if you can have him on a week's trial. When you are reasonably certain that this is the horse you want to own, tell the vendor that you will have the horse subjected to an examination by your veterinarian. Remember, the more horses you see and try, the better able you are to make comparisons; it is always a buyer's market.

The veterinarian will hopefully give you a written report that he has "examined the horse and found no clinical signs of disease, injury or physical abnormality which would be likely to affect its usefulness for the purpose for which the purchaser has informed him he is buying it".

The old adage of *caveat emptor* – "Let the buyer beware" – always applies. The purchaser is presumed to know exactly what he is buying and if he later finds that he was mistaken, or that his purchase suffers from some defect of which he was not aware, then the loss falls on him without the right of redress against the vendor.

Finally, before actually parting with your money, make sure the vendor has given you the appropriate papers. In most countries, a horse will have a registration certificate if he is registered with one of the breed societies. In addition, he should have current certificates of inoculations against tetanus and influenza.

Above left: Does he move straight or throw out a leg perhaps? You will be able to see this as he trots towards you.

Below: Ride him out of the yard and down the road to see whether he "naps", or is unwilling to leave the stable.

Above: Have him walked away from you in a straight line so that you can assess his action from behind.

Correctly-fitting tack is essential for the safety and well-being of both horse and rider. This is a Pelham bridle with curb chain, lip strap and double reins.

Saddles and bridles, with their various component parts – bits, stirrups, girths and the like – have become so much a part of riding life that most people seldom give them a thought. These and other ancillary items are loosely referred to as "tack" as opposed to "harness" which covers those items used on the driving horse.

Three thousand years of bits

Early horsemen acquired a degree of control over their horses by fixing a form of noseband around the jaw to which they attached reins. The Syrians, for example, are known to have used this system in the fourteenth century BC. However, there is evidence that a form of bridle incorporating something akin to a snaffle bit was used even earlier – in 1600 BC.

As riding became more widespread and common, so more and more ideas for "control" came into being. In about 800 BC, the Assyrians – by now experienced and accomplished horsemen – devised a more elaborate and forceful bridle, introducing a vicious forerunner of the drop noseband. This was a spiked strap which fastened tightly around the nose below the bit and which must have produced both pain and fear in their horses. Later, the famous Greek military commander and expert horseman, Xenophon, developed an early form of mouthing bit when he recommended that "short lengths of chain should be attached to the mouthpiece for the horse to pursue with his tongue". Not long after this, a ring bit was being used in Africa.

For a time, it seemed the trend was towards more severe bitting arrangements. From the sixth century BC onward, the Greeks and the Persians used spiked mouthpieces. The Celts of Gaul introduced the curb bit in around 400 BC, and this was still finding favor among the armored knights of the Middle Ages as they rode, in a somewhat cumbersome fashion, on the heavy horses needed to carry the weight of their armor. Much use of the curb was made during the Renaissance period, when school riding became popular and an exaggerated, rather over-bent head carriage was the vogue.

The curb bit came in various guises, but as a general rule it comprised very long cheeks and a thin mouthpiece. By and large, it was the way used to "break the animal's resistance by forceful means", once thought to be the right way to master the horse. The early Italian riding masters – Grisone and, later, Pignatelli – did place an emphasis on "preserving the lightness of the mouth", but presumably this was at the expense of the poor animal's nose, for they reintroduced the use of the spiked noseband.

Xenophon's early mouthing bit also came into use again. Perhaps recognition had come that, in order to achieve that over-bent head carriage so much admired, it was necessary for a horse to produce saliva, done by "mouthing" the bit, in order for his lower jaw to relax and the poll to flex.

The curb bit continued its popularity right through to the eighteenth century while classical riding remained the most popular riding activity. When hunting and a generally "freer" form of riding became more fashionable during the nineteenth and twentieth centuries, less stress was placed on the head position, and numerous milder bits were introduced.

Today, a bridle is generally classified by the type (or absence) of its bit and there are five basic groups. These are the *snaffle*, the *double bridle*, the *Pelham*, the *gag* and the *bitless*.

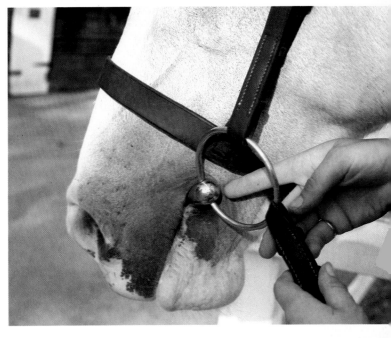

Above: A correctly-fitting loose ring snaffle. The ring must be well clear of the sides of the mouth to prevent pinching; this danger is reduced with a fixed ring.

Snaffle

Mildest of all these and the one most generally in use is the snaffle, of which there are a number of types. As a general rule, the thicker the mouthpiece of the bit, the milder is the action. Snaffle bits may have a straight or "half-moon" (slightly curved) mouthpiece or a jointed mouthpiece. The latter type tend to be a little more severe as the two halves can exercise a squeezing action across the lower jaw, known as "nutcracker" action.

The mildest jointed snaffle is the German snaffle, which has a thick, wide mouthpiece with a center hollow to reduce the weight on the tongue. The bit rings may be either fixed or loose; the former – the most common type being the eggbutt – is less likely to pinch the corners of the mouth.

The action of the snaffle depends on the horse's state of training. In a young, unschooled horse, whose head carriage tends to be low, the action is an upward one on the corners of the mouth, while on a more highly schooled horse whose head carriage is higher, the action will be on the bars of the mouth and the lower jaw.

The double bridle, known also as the Weymouth, probably comprises the most sophisticated bitting arrangement for it has two bits, and so two sets of reins. To a certain extent, these should be operated independently. The bits are the bridoon – the name given to the snaffle in this instance – and the curb bit, which consists of a straight mouthpiece with a hump in the middle to accommodate the tongue. The severity – or otherwise – of the curb depends on the length of the cheek below the mouthpiece; the longer it is, the more severe will be the effect. It is used with a curb chain (a metal-linked chain that hooks onto either side of the mouthpiece and fits into the outside groove of the horse's chin) and a lip strap. The curb chain exerts pressure on the lower jaw when applied from the rein, and the thin leather lip strap keeps the curb chain in place.

The action of the double bridle is two-fold; the bridoon raises the head while the curb causes a flexion of the poll and lower jaw and helps to lower the nose. It is used particularly in dressage and advanced schooling and, because of its complexity, should only be used by an educated rider and an already well-trained horse.

Below: A gag bridle is the most severe bit. Although this bridle has not been treated, new leather should always be oiled or greased before being used to prevent cracking.

The Pelham could be described as being a compromise double bridle, aiming in general to combine the actions of both bits in just one. Great numbers of Pelham bits exist, however, some with a port (raised part in the middle of the mouthpiece) and some without, and each is used for a different reason. Common among them are the Kimblewick, which is unusual in that it has no cheek pieces below the mouthpiece so instead has D-shaped rings somewhat like a snaffle; the Scamperdale, which consists of a straight metal bar and is a common one for strong little ponies and the Vulcanite, which is probably the mildest. Two reins should be used with a Pelham bit for the greatest effect; however, it is commonly used on ponies ridden by young children who find it difficult to cope with a two-rein handful, so short leather straps known as roundings, couplings, joiners or bit converters can be useful. These are joined to the two bit rings and the reins are connected to them.

The gag is the most severe of all bits and should only be used by experienced horsemen who have an extremely good reason for wanting this drastic form of control. The mouthpiece is basically a snaffle to which a rein is attached, but another rein leads from the cheekpieces, which are rounded at the lower end, to pass through two slots positioned at the top and bottom of the bit rings. This is known as the gag rein which exerts forceful pressure on the head; even when a gag is being worn, the gag rein should only be used when necessary.

As its name implies, the bitless bridle has no bit at all and control over the horse is achieved through exerting pressure on a noseband which is padded. It is a useful bridle to use on a horse with a mouth injury or one with a mouth that has become insensitive through bad riding. However, it is not as mild as it might seem, and indeed, some types of bitless bridle can be extremely severe. They should be used only by experienced hands.

All bits act on one or more parts of the horse's head:
Snaffle – an upward action on the corners of the mouth.
Double – basically an upward action through the bridoon on the corners of the mouth and a downward action through the curb on the bars, curb groove and poll.
Pelham – an upward action on the corners of the mouth and a downward action on the tongue, bars, curb groove and poll.
Gag – an upward action on the corners of the mouth and downward action on the poll.
Bitless – a downward action on the nose, poll and curb groove.
The only other area with which a bit could come into contact is the roof of the mouth and this could only happen in the case of a curb bit with a very high port. However, this should never be allowed to occur.

Above: A well-fitting bitless bridle, which works by a downward action on the nose.

Below: A flash noseband closes the mouth and prevents the horse from crossing his jaw.

Above: A correctly-fitted drop noseband. It should be high enough so as not to interfere with the horse's breathing.

Below: An Irish martingale, designed to prevent the reins from coming over the horse's head if the rider falls off.

The Bridle

Whatever size bridle is necessary to fit the horse and whatever the bit being used, the bridle consists of the same component parts. These are:

The headpiece or *crownpiece* – a strap that fits over the horse's head behind the ears onto which the cheek-pieces (see below) buckle and which incorporates the *throatlatch.* This long thin strap goes under the horse's throat, buckles on the near side (left) and keeps the bridle from slipping over the horse's head in the event of an accident.

The browband – a narrow strip that slots onto the headpiece and goes in front of the horse's ears, to keep the headpiece from slipping back. It is important that the browband is big enough, otherwise it will pinch the horse's ears.

The cheekpieces or *cheekstraps* – straps that buckle on either side of the bridle to the headpiece and, at the lower end, onto the bit rings. They must be adjusted to ensure that the bit lies in the correct position in the mouth, just against the corners.

The noseband – the band that goes around the nose, with a strap that runs over the top of the head to keep it in place. Various styles and types are available (see below), and fitting the noseband depends a little on which type is used.

The reins – straps fastened to the bit rings and providing the rider's contact with the horse's mouth.

As suggested above, there are various types of nosebands, as there are, too, different types of reins. The plain *cavesson* noseband is generally the most commonly seen, but in fact it serves very little useful purpose, except to improve the look of the horse's head. He will look "undressed" without it. The sheepskin-covered noseband, originally devised for use on America's trotting horses, and most frequently seen on racehorses today, also does not have a great practical use, although it was devised to restrict the horse's vision and prevent him from seeing something out of the corner of his eye which might cause him to shy off course. Today, blinkers are more generally used if this could be a danger. Nosebands that have a more positive purpose and are widely used are the *drop noseband,* the *Grackle* or *Figure Eight* and the *Flash.* Each of these has a refined use, but in general they are designed to close the horse's mouth, preventing him from crossing his jaw or opening the mouth in an effort to evade the bit. They must be fitted sufficiently high on the nose in order not to interfere with breathing.

Types of reins include those of plain leather, plaited or braided leather, plain leather with V-shaped thin leather strips placed at intervals along the length of the rein, and leather with a strip of "pimple" rubber covering them. The last two in particular are designed to help prevent them from slipping through the rider's hands when riding in wet weather conditions. Reins can also be made of plaited nylon, or webbing – the latter again usually have small V-shaped leather strips at intervals.

Horses who have a tendency to carry their heads in an unacceptably high position, so that they evade the bit and lessen the rider's control, may well require a *martingale*. Varieties in most common use are the standing and the running martingale. The standing martingale is attached to a cavesson or Flash noseband (never a drop noseband as the pressure would affect the horse's breathing) at one end and the girth at the other. It is kept in place by a neckstrap. It exerts pressure on the nose, thus helping to keep the head down and in, and it should be adjusted so that it forms a straight line from girth to noseband when the head is carried in the correct position. The running martingale is connected to the reins (it has a divided strap, each with a ring through which the reins are passed) and brings the head down by exerting pressure on the mouth through the reins. It should be adjusted so that the reins run in a straight line from the bit to the rider's hands when his hands and the horse's head are in the correct position. It can be extremely severe if it is adjusted too tightly.

Two other martingales in less common use are the *Market Harborough* and the *Irish*. The former is only used on very headstrong horses. It applies pressure on the bars of the mouth when the horse throws his head up; when he holds it in the correct position, as with the other two types already described, its action does not come into play. The Irish martingale is not a genuine martingale; it comprises a short strip of leather with a ring on either end through which the reins pass just behind the bit. Its primary use is to stop the reins from coming over the horse's head in the event of a fall and it is used mainly in racing, where this is a frequent danger.

Curb chains and lip straps, mentioned earlier, are really intrinsically part of a double or pelham bridle. Curb chains can be either single or double linked, and although most are usually made of metal, they can also be leather or elastic to prevent possible chafing. The links should lie flat in the curb groove and the chain should never be so tight that it pinches the skin.

Below: A running martingale, which connects the girth to the reins by a divided leather strap, brings the head down by exerting downward pressure on the horse's mouth.

The Saddle

Generations of horsemen improvised some sort of covering to make sitting on the horse's back more comfortable. The Assyrians in the ninth century BC (like the American Indians of later times) used a padded cloth, without girth or stirrups, and they were by no means alone in trying to find something to make riding a less bruising activity.

It seems that the first padded saddle was developed in the Ukraine in the fifth century BC and consisted of two hide cushions stuffed with horse hair and joined together across the spine with a leather strap. Besides making the rider more comfortable, it improved life for the horse too, for it had the effect of spreading the rider's weight across the spine. It was followed some 700 years later by the wooden saddle, and then by the wooden raised-base saddle which was covered in hide and raised at either end – the pommel and cantle as we know them today. Medieval knights heightened the pommel and cantle even further to help keep them in the saddle during the impact of the charge. During the Renaissance period, when school-riding was all the vogue, the saddle became padded, still with a raised pommel and cantle.

Credit for the invention of the stirrup, a development that made the rider more secure and allowed greater movement in the saddle that in turn improved fighting techniques, goes to the mounted bowman Huns of Mongolia. In its basic form it comprised a rope for the toe, a somewhat unstable piece of equipment.

Styles of riding have necessarily influenced designs of saddles. Jumping had played no part in cavalry maneuvers until Italian cavalry officer Federico Caprilli (1868-1908) realized that reconnaissance troops would be more effective if they did not have to go round the small obstacles that lay in their way across a given route.

In order to accommodate jumping over these in safety, he developed the "forward system" of riding, which required horse and rider to "acquire free natural balance under all conditions". This necessitated the rider sitting slightly more forward in the saddle than he had been used to and riding with a shorter stirrup leather. The riding style of today, at least in European or English seat riding, is basically a compromise between the classical style of school riding and Caprilli's forward seat, and saddlery has developed accordingly.

Left: Today's saddles have come a long way from the padded cloths used by early Assyrian horsemen in the ninth century BC. The essential purpose of the saddle is to give the rider security and more control. This shows the correct way to carry a saddle.

The essential purpose of the saddle in all styles or forms of riding is to make it more comfortable, giving the rider greater security, and thus greater control. To this end, the saddle must fit both horse and rider. This is achieved by the fact that the "tree" – that is the frame around which the saddle is built – comes in three width fittings, narrow, medium and broad, and four lengths ranging from 15 ins (38 cm) to 17½ in (44 cm). The saddle must be high enough and wide enough to clear the horse's backbone and the withers. The rider should be able to insert three fingers (held vertically) between the pommel and the withers, and it should be wide enough to ensure that it does not pinch just below the withers or anywhere along the spine.

The saddle tree was traditionally made of beech wood, but plastic, fiberglass and laminated wood are all used nowadays. There are two principal types – the rigid tree, and the spring tree which has two steel springs inserted underneath the rear along the seat and makes the saddle more comfortable for the rider. The saddle should be big enough for the rider to sit comfortably in the center, without making contact with the pommel or the cantle, and should not be so wide that his legs stretch uncomfortably across it.

The exact type of saddle a rider chooses depends upon the type of riding activity he mainly pursues, for differing designs have been evolved to suit different equestrian disciplines. The extremes are the dressage saddle, designed to show off the horse's shoulder and to put the rider's weight very slightly to the rear, and the racing saddle, designed to put minimum weight on the horse's back and to carry the rider's weight well forward. These two apart, there are perhaps two other main types of saddle; that designed for show-jumping, and the one in the most common use, the general purpose saddle, designed for ordinary leisure riding, long-distance trail riding, cross-country riding and hunting.

Most saddles (specialist types such as the racing saddle excluded) have a central "dip" to the seat and knee rolls, which vary in thickness according to the principal use of the saddle, but which are designed to support the thigh just above the knee. The position of the stirrup bars to which the stirrup leathers is attached is further back in a dressage saddle and this also has a straight or cut-back head, and relatively straight flaps. Most dressage saddles have two girth straps instead of the usual three, and these are much longer, extending below the end of the flap. This means the rider has the minimum amount of leather "bulk" between himself and his horse, so the lightest, most subtle of aids can still be interpreted. Most jumping and general purpose saddles are built on a spring tree; the difference between them lies mainly in the shape of the flap – the general purpose is cut straighter than the jumping saddle. The head is usually sloped (as opposed to cut-back or vertical) in both instances, allowing the stirrup bars to be placed further forward.

Above: A breastplate can be used on a horse whose saddle tends to slide backwards.

Below: This is a dressage saddle. Note the distinctive straight-cut flap.

Saddle accessories

The saddle is held in place on the horse's back by the girth – of which there are three common forms, the *Balding, Atherstone* and *three-fold*. The Balding and the Atherstone are shaped so as to be narrower in the center portion, where they lie behind the horse's elbows, and wider at either end where they buckle onto the straps of the saddle. The Balding divides into three equal strips which are plaited one on either side of the center piece, while the Atherstone is the same basic shape, but is not plaited and has an additional strip of leather down the center. Both of these girths are useful for a horse that is sensitive-skinned and prone to girth galls as they lessen any likelihood of chafing. The three-fold, as its name implies, comprises one strip of leather which is folded over three times. The folded edge lies behind the horse's forelegs, to minimize the risk of chafing. Besides leather, girths can also be made of "lampwick" (a soft fabric) or nylon cord, the cheapest of all materials.

Stirrup leathers are usually made of strong cowhide which tends to stretch less than other leathers. However, all leather stretches to some extent, and it is a good idea, therefore, to change over the leathers to opposite sides of the saddle fairly frequently so as they stretch to the same extent. The near-side leather will stretch to a greater degree because it is the one used for mounting.

Stirrup irons are made most satisfactorily of stainless steel; nickel ones will be cheaper but are more likely to bend and even break. Three main types of stirrup iron are in common use – the ordinary *plain iron*, the *Kournakoff* and the *child's safety iron*, or *Peacock iron*. The plain iron is the one most frequently used and, as its name implies, is perfectly straightforward. It requires only to be large enough to prevent the rider's foot getting stuck in it. The Kournakoff has sloping sides, and a tread that slopes upwards; the slot for the stirrup leather is placed slightly askew which helps to position the rider's toe up and his heel down.

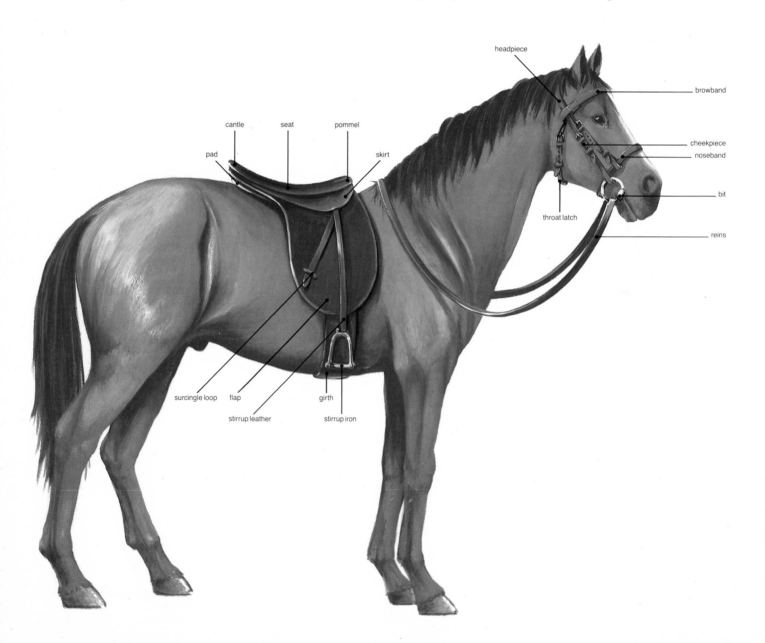

In a Peacock iron, the metal edge is replaced by a thick rubber band which stretches over a hook at the top and bottom. The idea is that in the event of a fall, the rubber comes undone for easy release of the foot. Rubber treads or "stirrup pads" can be fitted onto the tread of the stirrup iron (whatever the type) and are useful as an anti-slip device.

Numnahs or saddle pads are frequently seen in use under a saddle and may be made of sheepskin, nylon-simulated sheepskin or cotton-covered foam. They are saddle-shaped and are generally held in place by tapes or leather or nylon fastenings. They can be used to give added protection to a thin-coated or clipped back, but they cannot change a badly-fitting saddle into one that fits well. If used, they must be kept clean or a sore back will soon result. They should be pushed right up into the channel of the saddle; if stretched across the horse's back they will exert pressure and friction on the spine.

Below: A variety of saddles, some with numnahs, cleaned and stored correctly on saddle racks. Saddles should not be left standing on end as this can weaken the tree.

Right: A tack room should be kept neat and tidy and tack regularly cleaned. Here bridles are correctly hung up, reins through the throatlash, after being cleaned.

70

Cleaning tack

All tack becomes dirty with use; mud and dirt from wet trails and fields collects on the leather, together with grease and sweat from the horse's skin, and these will harden into places that will quicky cause rubbing. In addition, leather needs "feeding" if it is not to dry out and harden or crack. Regular and thorough cleaning is essential.

Saddles should be stripped – that is the girth, stirrup leathers and irons must be removed – and bridles dismantled completely, so that each part can be cleaned individually. All leather should be wiped over with lukewarm, not hot, water and a damp sponge, taking care to remove all dirty deposits. When it has dried, saddle soap should be rubbed in with a slightly damp sponge; this rubbing should be sufficient to produce a shine! A check should be made at this time to make sure the leather is in good condition, without any general signs of wear, loose stitching and so on.

New leather should be greased or oiled before being used, and it is a good idea to repeat this from time to time, particularly if it is not in regular use, or if it is to be stored for some time.

If girths are not made of leather, they should be scrubbed and left to dry. Careful attention should be paid to girths (which should be cleaned after every use); they are most likely to collect deposits of mud which, if these are left to harden, will quickly cause girth galls. Stirrup irons and bits should be washed; the irons and bit rings can be polished with metal polish. Again, clean off any saliva deposits on bits every time they have been used, otherwise they will harden and scratch the corners of the mouth.

Below: Tack cleaning in progress. Saddle soap is used to give the tack a shine and help preserve the leather.

Horse clothing

In addition to the tack required for riding purposes, most horses will need certain other items of equipment and clothing. For example, in order to secure him for grooming, shoeing, visits from the veterinarian or for traveling, he will need a headcollar or halter. The strongest and smartest ones, perhaps, are the leather ones, but extremely tough nylon ones are also available.

A stabled horse, particularly if the weather is cold or he has a thin coat or has been clipped, will need to wear a night rug or blanket. These are traditionally made of canvas or jute with a warm woollen lining. Some have surcingles sewn onto them to keep them in place, or a separate surcingle or roller may be used for this purpose. In very cold weather, it may be necessary to provide a blanket or two under the rug. Night rugs are now made in quilted nylon with a polyester fiber filling, and lined with brushed nylon or some sort of cotton-based fabric, or they may be made with a detachable acrylic fiber pile lining and a synthetic waterproof outer covering so that, in theory anyway, they can be worn both in the stable and when the horse is turned out in the field for a few hours. These are known as "turnout" rugs. It is still perhaps more usual for a horse to be turned out in the heavy New Zealand rug, or one similar, made of waterproof canvas with adjustable hindleg straps designed to prevent the rug from slipping. These should never be worn in the stable, however cold the weather.

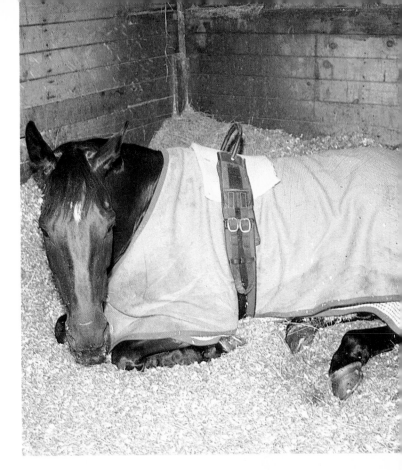

Above: A horse, stabled on shavings, wearing a jute night rug to keep warm in winter.

Below left: A wool day rug keeps the horse warm when at a show and for traveling.

Below: A New Zealand rug is worn when the horse is turned outdoors. Here the leg straps have been correctly linked through each other to keep the rug in place.

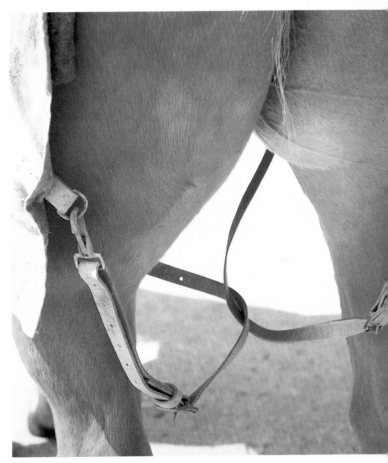

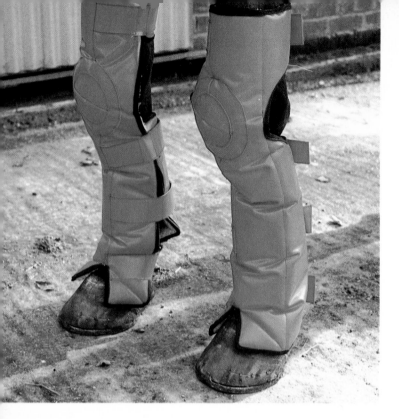

Above: Leg protectors, the modern all-in-one kneecaps and bandages to protect the horse's legs when traveling.

A horse who has sweated up during strenuous exercise should wear an anti-sweat rug which allows him to dry off without getting cold. An anti-sweat rug looks like a cotton string vest, and in fact is really only effective if a light blanket or sheet is placed over the top of it, so that insulating air pockets are created. In cold weather, when traveling to or waiting around at a show, a woollen day rug or blanket can be worn. These come in various colors and are bound in a contrasting color, often with the owner's initials displayed, also in the contrasting color. If the day is warm, a cotton summer sheet will replace the woollen rug; this also helps to keep the coat lying flat and free from dust.

Besides a rug of some sort, when traveling the horse must wear some form of protection on his legs. Woollen stable bandages wound over thick gamgee tissue protect the leg from knee to coronet (they can also be used for warmth and protection in the stable when necessary) and knee pads will prevent any knocks to the knee. Knee pads comprise leather-bound woollen "squares" with a central leather pad and are fastened round the leg with straps above and below the knee. Special ones are available to wear on exercise if the horse is prone to stumbling, or is so valuable that he must be protected against all eventualities. Those horses likely to bump their hocks while traveling will also need to wear hock boots which are made and operate on a similar principal. In recent times, "all-in-one" traveling boots or leg protectors have become available on the market; they obviate the need for bandages and knee and hock boots, since they comprise protection for the leg from hock or knee right down over the pastern. They are made of foam rubber or PVC with a fur fabric lining and fasten with Velcro.

Always when traveling, and often in the stable, a horse should wear a tail bandage to prevent the tail being rubbed, or simply to keep a neatly groomed tail tidy. If the horse is particularly prone to rubbing his tail by scraping against the upturned ramp of the trailer, he should wear a tail guard, a rectangular piece of leather, canvas or wool which is fastened over the tail bandage. For horses that are likely to throw their heads up, so that they might receive a bad knock, a poll-guard or head bumper may also be necessary. This is a thick, half-moon-shaped piece of felt with a leather backing which fits on to the headcollar and sits on the poll.

Horses who tend to throw their legs about when being exercised may well need some protection from bangs and blows. Stretchy elastic bandages wound over gamgee tissue from below the knee to above the fetlock joint will help to protect this area of the leg (and will also give support to the tendons, useful for horses in heavy competitive work or if the ground is very hard). Brushing and over-reach boots protect the legs from knocks given with the other front or hind leg, and from injury caused by the hindleg striking the heels of the forelegs, respectively.

Brushing boots generally comprise an oval-shaped piece of felt with a shaped leather reinforcement to cover the fetlock area and are kept in place by leather straps. Plastic and nylon boots are also on the market. There are two types of over-reach boots; a grooved circular rubber one which is pulled on over the hoof, and one with an opening down one side with a leather strap which fits through D rings, making it easier to put on and take off. Over-reach injuries are common in show-jumpers, when the tendency is for the hind legs to strike the forelegs when landing over a jump. Tendon boots, a longer version of the brushing boot, are useful in those horses who knock themselves with the other leg higher up and schooling boots, made of PVC with Velcro fastenings, are useful to give protection to the legs and support to the tendons of a youngster in his early training days.

Above: Rubber over-reach boots, often seen on show-jumpers, who are likely to overreach when landing over a jump.

A Continental form of poll guard which fits onto the headcollar, used on horses which tend to throw their heads up and suffer knocks when traveling.

Up to a certain point, the training of the horse could be likened to the schooling of the human child, and, of course, it is just as necessary.

Clearly, differences exist between the two. Because of the horse's shorter life span (two-thirds less than that of the human), the schooling has to be condensed into a correspondingly shorter period of time, and it is naturally concerned far more with physical development than intellectual improvement. Even so, the mental conditioning of the horse and the extension of his powers of concentration plays just as important a part in his training – running, in fact, almost parallel with his physical education.

No responsible person would deny the value of a sound education to the human child. It is, indeed, essential to life in our society. Whether the training of the horse is considered in the same light is by no means so certain; it should be, though, for it is upon the schooling he receives that the horse's happy and useful future depends. Indeed, it is not too much to say that the horse's working life can be prolonged by correct and progressive physical conditioning in his basic education, allowing him to perform more effectively and with less risk of strain to limbs and organs, *and* with less likelihood of mental stress.

Schooling the horse is the way to develop his natural powers. The next stage is for them to be directed towards the purposes which are required of him and to which he seems best suited. During the process it will be necessary to subjugate some of his natural instincts, which are not always very helpful to us as riders. The horse has to be taught, for example, to obey the requests of his rider up to the point where he can even overcome his dominant "herd-instinct". The trained horse will leave the collecting ring and the magnetic presence of other horses (his temporary herd) to jump a course on his own, away from his companions, in the show jumping arena.

Show jumping is a major example of training overcoming the natural instinct to remain in the group or herd. Course-builders, understanding this, will erect, particularly for novice horses, the easier, more encouraging fences in the early part of the course, reserving the more difficult ones for the latter part when the horse will be heading towards the collecting ring and his companions and will benefit from what might be called their "gravitational pull".

Subjugation can never be total, nor should it be, for then there would be a danger of breaking the horse's spirit and reducing him to a dull, mindless automaton. It can only be achieved within reasonable and acceptable limits and it is accomplished by the horse acquiring, through training, the habit of willing obedience and immediate physical response to a set of

Left: Top eventer Richard Meade clearing a fence on Kilcashel. It takes years of progressive schooling to excel in eventing.

signals (called "aids") made by the rider's limbs and body. These aids are in effect the language of riding and become the means of communication between horse and rider.

It is, of course, up to the human member of the partnership to teach the horse this body-language. It is not something which the horse naturally understands. The first time a rider squeezes a horse with his legs, the accepted signal to move forwards, there is no reason for the horse to have any idea what it is that is expected of him. He has to be taught to associate the squeeze with the action of moving forward until it becomes a sort of conditioned reflex. (It follows, of course, that until the rider has learned these accepted aids, he or she cannot hope to teach them to a horse, but more of that in the following chapter.)

The horse's training can be divided into four parts, and this applies just as much in general principle to Western riding as to the Eastern or European style. There are differences between the two in respect of the way in which some movements are performed, in the bitting arrangements involved, and while jumping is very much a part of Eastern riding it has no place in the schooling of the Western horse, since it is not relevant to the work he will be asked to perform.

EDUCATION IN FOUR STAGES

The initial stage in training is that of the nursery school, which takes the horse from birth to about three years. This is followed by a period of primary education which may last for no more than six months, after which the horse is given a rest and allowed time to grow naturally, the growth being encouraged by good feeding. At the age of four the secondary stage is begun. Although still far from being mature, most horses will then be sufficiently developed and strong enough to be given somewhat more demanding exercises.

For most horses the formal education stops here, but there will be gifted performers who will be able to go on to higher, "university" level education and specialize in one or other of the main disciplines.

In Eastern riding, horses can be schooled in dressage, show jumping or eventing, taking them into international competition. In Western riding there are equivalent specialist pursuits. All horses, however, should be able to attain a reasonable standard at a secondary level if their training has been conducted intelligently.

At the end of the secondary stage it would be expected that a well-developed young horse schooled for the Eastern requirement should, by reason of his training, be comfortable and obedient to ride. He should be able to compete satisfactorily in jumping and dressage competitions at a preliminary or even medium level and he should be able to cope with the cross-country course at a one-day horse trials event.

Much of the nursery stage is concerned with the young foal learning by association with his dam and by copying her. Certainly only minimal demands are made of the youngster during this stage and none which call for physical effort on his part.

The immediate objectives, beyond the natural development of the foal, are concerned with forming a relationship between man and the animal and then, once the foal's confidence has been won, introducing an element of discipline which enables the first very simple lessons in obedience to be taught. This will involve the foal accepting the presence of humans and becoming accustomed to being handled by them. In both of these, the foal will follow the example of the mare and if she submits easily to handling there should be no difficulty in his following her example. Thereafter, there is no great problem involved in fitting a halter on the foal and teaching him to lead in hand, but this needs to be approached in easy stages.

Handling of the foal will begin in the field where he will be turned out with his dam. Given that she is calm and trustful of human beings, there should be no difficulty in stroking, patting and scratching the youngster. Scratching is an imitation of the natural behavioral pattern of the horse, and foals obviously enjoy it, particularly when it is done on the chest, over the withers and just above the juncture of the tail with the body.

When it comes to putting a halter on the foal, it is easiest to do this in the stable. To this end, mare and foal should be brought in each day. The whole business of handling the foal is based largely on the fact that the youngster will always follow his mother, so once the mare is caught and led to the stable the foal should simply follow.

Haltering is the first major step in the education of the young horse and should be carried out quietly, firmly and by gradual steps. It if becomes a battle, with the handlers resorting to force, the foal will be frightened and subsequent training will be unnecessarily difficult.

The first step is to place the mare against a wall with the foal standing at her side. The handler then encircles the foal with his arms, one round the chest and one round the quarters. After a day or two the foal will accept the encircling arms without seeking to escape. It is then possible to have the mare led round the box with the foal being encouraged to follow within the cradling arms. A push on his quarters will send him forward and the arm round the chest can act to restrain any over-enthusiastic plunge. Once the exercise is established, the left arm, the one held round the chest, can be replaced by a soft stable-rubber (the linen grooming-cloth) put around the foal's neck. Using the cloth and the forward-pushing arm around the quarters, the foal can then be led to and from the field.

Fitting the halter

The foal is now properly prepared for the fitting of the halter. Do not try to rush this stage; it is this constant preparation of the horse by progressive stages which is at the root of all successful training methods. To fit the halter, or foal slip, two people are needed. One positions the foal, encircling the quarters with his right arm, while the other, holding the slip open with a cheekpiece in each hand, slips the nosepiece behind the ears and fastens it to the cheekpiece.

It is quite possible that the foal will attempt to run backwards or even rear, but a gentle push from the arm around the quarters will send him forward into the halter. This is the *right* way: the *wrong* way is to try to push the halter onto the foal.

With a little encouragement from behind combined with a gentle pull on the halter, the foal will soon learn to walk around the stables. This is an opportunity for the foal to learn that he has to respond to verbal commands, too. Each time he is asked to move forward one or other of the helpers gives the command "walk-on" (or something similar) a second or so before the physical pull and push. The foal learns to relate the command to the required movement and is taught a valuable lesson. Within a short time it should be possible to lead the foal outside by his halter, initially with two helpers and then with one.

Left: Nursery school training starts from when the foal is born, to form a relationship between horse and rider that becomes the basis of future discipline and obedience.

During all this training, though, use should be made of the mare's presence.

At this point, a considerable amount has been achieved. The foal has grown accustomed to humans, he has learned to submit, to accept the halter and to walk in-hand (led by the halter), and he has learned to respond to at least one verbal command.

The training can be carried a stage further by picking up his feet (in preparation for when the farrier fits shoes in the future) and it should also be possible after hand-rubbing the head and body to groom the foal very gently with a very soft brush. If the foal is allowed to watch the mare being groomed and having her feet picked up and attended to and sees that she makes no fuss, he will usually follow suit.

Since most modern horses will have to travel in trailers and horse floats, young horses need to be introduced to these vehicles as early as possible so that they come to accept them as commonplace. It is always advisable when loading a mare and foal (the two cannot yet be separated) to load the foal first rather than the mare. Cradled between the arms of two helpers it is relatively easy to bundle the foal into the container, and the mare will immediately follow so as not to be separated from her offspring. If the mare is put in first, the foal, perhaps not being able to see his mother clearly, could panic and the mare, her protective instincts roused, would then rush out of the trailer to be with her foal.

Above: Early stages: the young horse wearing a roller, cavesson and lunge line.

Below: The young horse on the lunge in trot. The side reins are attached to the cavesson.

Opinions differ about the age at which the next stage of training, which we have called primary, should commence. Some people recommend beginning the schooling at two years, while others hold that it is better to wait until the age of three when the horse is stronger, more developed and less likely to suffer stress. The latter has some obvious merits and there are many horsemen who would hold that to allow the horse an extra year in which to grow naturally (or even two years if the animal is big and likely to mature late) pays dividends in the length of useful working life that can normally be expected.

It has to be remembered that the horse is not mature until he is four and a half years old, the time when his milk teeth are replaced by permanent ones. In the early training, therefore, we are really dealing with babies and, since their limbs and bone-structure are not fully formed, they can easily be damaged by injudicious work. The young horse should not be ignored between the time he is haltered until he reaches his third birthday; rather he needs to be handled continually, his feet need attention and it may even be possible to put a bit in his mouth.

The objectives of this further stage of training are to condition the horse to carry weight (i.e. the rider), then to get him used to working with the rider in the saddle and finally to teach him to respond to the elementary aids. Much of the time (and this stage of training need not extend much more than four or five months) is spent in "preparing" the horse, and considerable use is made of work on the lunge rein. Lunging, in the simplest terms, involves the horse moving in a circle round the trainer on the end of a long rein or line at a walk, trot and eventually at canter.

Above: Detail of the lunge cavesson with the lunge line attached to the central ring. The horse must learn to accept the tack in the stable before lunging is attempted.

The lunge rein

The rein, usually made of soft webbing, is about 27 ft. (8.2 m) in length and is fastened to a special lunge cavesson (strong head collar) fitted with rings on the nosepiece to which the rein is attached. The trainer, holding the rein across his body, encourages the horse to move forward by means of a long lunge whip held behind the horse. If the horse is moving on a left-handed circle the trainer holds the rein in his left hand, passing the slack across his body and into his right hand, which also holds the whip. On a circle to the right the opposite would apply.

Lunging acts as a strengthening and suppling exercise. It is also a means of calming the horse and, very importantly, it teaches the horse to go forward from the indications of the whip while establishing the habit of obedience to the voice, of which much use should be made. It serves, too, at a later stage as a basis for teaching the elementary aids under the rider, since with the horse on the lunge the rider's actions of leg and hand can initially be supported by the trainer's voice, and it is used in first jumping lessons as well.

A lot of the preparatory work for this primary training takes place not on the lunge rein, but in the stable, where the young horse has to get accustomed to being tied up, to being groomed, to having his feet picked up, and to learning stable manners.

It is in the stable, too, that he will be fitted with his lunge cavesson, and, later, a bit has to be put in his mouth. If time has been spent handling his head, particularly around the ears and mouth, the introduction of the bit – supported by cheekpieces and a headpiece – should present no difficulty. Usually, a piece of carrot held with the bit, and slipped into the mouth with it, ensures a trouble-free operation. The bit is then left in the mouth for an hour or so a day for the young horse to get used to it being there. If he is given a small feed, this encourages him to "mouth" the bit and relax his jaws. Some trainers use "breaking" bits which are fitted with "keys" set in the center of the mouthpiece. The "keys" encourage the horse to play with the bit and "mouth" it.

A roller, a wide leather or web band passing round the horse's girth and padded on each side of the wither, should also be fitted. This is a preparation for the fitting of the saddle.

Initially, this exercise period involves no more than the horse – wearing his cavesson and perhaps his roller – being led about for him to see what is going on. This leading in hand does, however, have a more serious purpose. It teaches the horse to go forward in response to his trainer's (or rider's) commands.

Going forward is the first requirement of any riding horse and is an absolute priority of his training. When a horse ceases to go forward in response to either the voice and the indications made by the whip (a horse is not struck with the latter, punishment with the whip being only an extremely rare occurrence) or the use of the rider's leg he becomes, quite simply, out of control and the rider is at his mercy. Taken to the extreme, a refusal to jump fences occurs only because a horse has ceased to go forward at a signal from the rider's legs.

To begin with, a trainer can make use of an assistant to teach the horse to move forward freely in hand. He positions himself at the horse's left (near-side) shoulder holding the rein, attached to the cavesson ring, in his right hand, the slack being taken across the body to the opposite hand in which he holds a long schooling whip. The schooling whip is shorter than a lunge whip, but of sufficient length so that it can be held behind the back and tapped on the horse's flank when necessary.

The trainer then gives the command "walk-on", accompanying the instruction with a tap from the whip. As a further encouragement his assistant may walk up behind the horse. Very quickly the horse learns to go forward on the command and the whip tap. He should be taught to stop by the command "whoa", the trainer checking on the rein at the same time as giving the command.

Right: This is the sort of easy, long-striding walk which is expected and encouraged in the early stages of training; the horse moves freely, without any restriction.

Left: The horse being worked on the lunge at a walk. Note how the side reins are adjusted loosely to encourage the horse to stretch into contact with them.

Protective boots

The step from leading in-hand to lunging is a simple one. It merely involves the trainer lengthening his rein, stepping back a stride or two and sending the horse forward with a movement of the lunge whip. The horse needs to wear protective boots on all four legs when worked on the lunge, since coordination is not yet well established in a young animal, and he can easily damage himself by striking one leg with another. It is possible that when lunging begins an assistant may be needed to lead the horse around the trainer who can also be helpful in teaching obedience to the simple words of command. As the trainer gives the commands to go forward, he should accompany them by an appropriate movement of the lunge whip.

Wise trainers almost always begin the lunge lesson on the right rein (i.e. the circle to the right). The reason for this is that it is more difficult for the horse (who has always been handled and led from the near side) and often more difficult for the trainer, too, to work on the right rein than on the left. The inclination can then be to do too much work on the left rein and not enough on the right. If that is allowed to happen the horse's muscular structure will be built up unequally, and his suppleness will be one-sided. He will turn easily to the left but only with considerably more difficulty to the right: this tendency will become very much more

Above: Crossing a pole grid at a trot. The pace should be steady but active; this is an excellent balancing and suppling exercise and serves as an introduction to jumping.

Above right: Towards the end of his primary schooling the young horse can be lunged over a grid of cavalletti, initially at a walk and later at a steady trot.

apparent when he is worked under saddle and has to cope with the weight of a rider.

When the horse lunges easily to both sides, keeps out on the circle (i.e. does not keep coming in to the center) and obeys the voice, the paces can be improved (in terms of rhythm and balance) and the horse can be "brought together" in a better "outline" – making him appear more compact – by using what is often called lunging "tackle". Without the minimal restraint imposed by the tackle, lunging achieves very little beyond obedience to the voice, since the young horse is inevitably moving in his usual rather "loose" fashion. This means his head is probably being carried too high, his back is hollow rather than rounded and his hindlegs tend to trail behind him rather than being used well under his body to push him forward with maximum effect. He is not using his body fully, and that is what the lunge tackle seeks to remedy.

Lunge tackle

The tackle consists of the cavesson, from which a bit can be suspended, the roller, which is fitted with rings on each side set at different heights, a pair of side-reins, short reins which can be attached either to the cavesson or to the bit rings and then back through the rings onto the roller, and a crupper. A crupper is a thick padded leather loop placed under the dock and connected by a strap to the back of the roller.

The reins, first fitted to the cavesson and then to the bit, are adjusted loosely to begin with, the horse being encouraged to "stretch" into contact with them. This can best be accomplished by first walking, then trotting, the horse over a grid of heavy poles laid on the ground at between 4 to 6 ft (1.2 to 1.5 m) apart – the distance varying according to the size and length of stride taken by the individual animal. Before laying out a series of poles the horse should be lunged at a walk, and then a trot, over a single pole, the grid being built up progressively from that point. The action of stepping over a pole causes the horse to lower his head and neck to operate the limbs more actively. In doing this he takes up the slack of the rein. It is also, incidentally, a very valuable strengthening exercise, for the hindlegs in particular.

The next step in the lunging procedure is to shorten the side reins, but not to the point of being taut, and not while asking the horse to continue the grid exercise, for he needs to be able to stretch out his neck to accomplish this effectively. Shortening the reins in conjunction with the crupper which holds the roller in place puts the lightest of contacts on the mouth.

From the lunge rein to the long reins is another comparatively easy transition to effect. An additional rein, similar to the lunge rein, is fastened to the outside ring of the cavesson (the ring farthest from the trainer), passed through one of the rings on the roller and then around the horse's quarters and back into the trainer's hand, the lunge rein remaining in its customary place. When the horse is working quietly in this arrangement the inside rein, the lunge rein, can be passed through the roller ring and back into the hand. It is now possible for an active person to drive the horse in circles or parts of circles to either hand and also to drive the horse forward from directly behind the quarters.

When the reins can be transferred to the bit rings it follows that the horse can be taught to respond to pressures on the mouth which cause him to turn, to halt, and even, with the help of an assistant, to take a few steps backwards.

The horse is now ready to be backed (have a saddle put on his back and a rider on top) with the rider in the saddle in control.

Saddling up

The saddle has first to be put on the horse's back, and this is usually done in the stable, after which the horse is lunged for a few days wearing the saddle. The feel of the saddle and particularly the creaking noise made by the leather sometimes upsets young horses and they need to be allowed to get used to it, so that they are working quietly in the saddle before a rider is first tried out on them.

Again, the backing process is best done for the first time in the stable, where the space is confined and there is less risk of an accident. Initially, the trainer, controlling the horse from a cavesson, helps the assistant to lie across the saddle, an exercise that can be done for a short time on two or three consecutive days. When the horse is clearly used to this, the rider puts a leg over his back and actually mounts into the saddle.

Left: Turning at the trot with the horse bent to the right, the head and neck correctly inclined towards the direction of the movement, with no resistance in the mouth.

Right: You can let the young horse negotiate a small jump while out on his daily ride.

Below: The cavalletti grid requires hard work and concentration by the horse.

Once settled with the rider on his back, the horse is made accustomed to the feel of the weight of the rider by being walked around the schooling area on the lunge. The reins held by the rider should be attached at first to the cavesson; later they can be moved to the bit.

Gradually, the control passes from the trainer to the rider. The horse has to learn to associate the action of the rider's legs, hands and body weight with the verbal commands, combined with a slight movement of the whip where applicable. The method employed is for the rider to squeeze with the legs just before the trainer's spoken command "walk-on" and the supporting movement made with the long whip. Very quickly the horse learns that the squeeze is the signal to go forward and just as easily he will learn the signals for trot, slow down and halt. The rider must be both competent and sensitive, someone who understands the aids and has learned how to apply them, as well as having a "feel" for riding and training a young horse.

For the rest of this primary stage the young horse learns how to carry the weight on his back, adjusting his balance accordingly. When it comes to riding out of the schooling area, it is best if the youngster can be accompanied by an older horse, from which he will gain confidence. Work and exercise should be done with the emphasis always on the horse going forward freely. It should take place in the open on tracks and trails and across fields, with little or no attempt to "school" the horse in circles or figures within an enclosed arena. At this stage such work would be too physically demanding for him. There is, however, no harm in letting a young horse, following after a more experienced one, hop over a log, a small bank, or cross a stream while out on his daily ride. Nor will it harm him to trot over a grid of poles every now and then. The important thing is to keep him interested, not do one thing repeatedly so that he becomes bored and his action mechanical and careless.

Jumping

Towards the end of this period there is no reason why the horse should not be lunged, unmounted, over one or two low obstacles. Jumping on the lunge allows the horse to develop his own initiative in the approach to the fence and helps him to judge distances for himself. He also learns to use himself over the jump without the inhibiting weight of the rider. Again, so as to have the freedom of his head and neck, the side-reins should not be fitted for jumping.

The piece of equipment used for these early jumping lessons and a follow-up to the poles on the ground is the "cavalletto", meaning "little horse". A cavalletto looks like a knife-rest made by a strong pole, about 10 ft (3 m) long, fixed between cross-struts at each end so that three separate heights can be obtained, depending on how the cavalletto rests on the ground. The lowest height is usually 10 in (25 cm), then 15 in (38 cm), then 19 in (48 cm).

Using a grid of four cavalletti placed at the same distance apart as previously set with the ground poles, the horse can first cross the grid at trot, at the lowest level, then the third cavalletto can be placed on top of the fourth to make a simple jump. All sorts of variations can be made by altering the heights and making use of the possible combinations.

Following the cavalletti exercises the horse (still on the lunge) can be asked to jump small fences, built as solidly as possible. An ideal arrangement for an early jumping exercise is to have an upright, not bigger than 2 ft 3 in (68 cm), on one side of the working area and a spread of 2 ft 6 in (76 cm) on the other. These fences provide differing problems, the first having to be jumped from a comparatively short stride and the second from a longer one which will act to increase the horse's scope (or range) over fences. These simple jumping exercises prepare the horse for jumping under a rider in the following secondary stage.

Right: The small fence of crossed poles placed at the end of the pole grid, which balances and steadies the horse in its approach, makes an excellent first fence.

2

1

Left: Crossing a pole grid at trot is a valuable exercise designed to assist the young horse in attaining a correct approach before tackling a small fence.

The usual custom at the conclusion of the primary period is, as suggested earlier, to give the horse a period of rest and relaxation, letting him get on with the business of growing and feeding accordingly.

SECONDARY TRAINING

The secondary stage begins possibly some months later when the horse is in his fourth year and is correspondingly more mature. No precise limit can be put on its duration but it is aimed at producing a physically strong horse well capable of competing in all disciplines at the "middle-of-the-road" level – a horse that is balanced, obedient, safe and comfortable to ride.

In effect, the ground work done in the primary stage is extended and refined in this stage, although, of course, new work has also to be done and the horse has to gain experience over a variety of obstacles.

The duration of daily work is increased gradually. At three years it would have been unwise to work the horse for more than an hour a day and, at the beginning of the training stage, 20 to 30 minutes would probably have been enough. Now it should be possible, over a period, to work up to as much as two hours a day.

Much of this work will be concerned with improving the balance by riding out across country, learning to jump small natural obstacles, to cross water and ditches and to work up and down slopes. In the jumping area of the schooling ground, fences should be made more varied and the problems of varying distances introduced. Fences remain low but are built in combinations and with increased spread.

Left: Note the distance pole placed on the ground before the jump, which checks the horse, helps him judge the fence and prevents him from rushing at it and becoming unbalanced.

3

4

Right: The horse making a good free jump over a small fence. The rider has allowed the rein to go loose, giving the horse freedom to stretch his neck over the jump.

Jumps and bounces

Two low vertical fences spaced at 24 ft (7.3 m) give, for instance, one non-jumping stride between them, where the horse, having landed over the first fence, has room to take just one full stride before taking off over the second element. To give two non-jumping strides between obstacles, the fences should be placed 33 ft (10 m) apart, and for three strides the distance is increased to 45 ft (13.7 m). Jumping such combinations will increase the horse's agility and confidence and as he gets more proficient, the "bounce" fence can be included. This comprises two solid fences placed 16 ft (4.8 m) apart so that the horse jumps the first then "bounces" over the second without there being a non-jumping stride between.

In the work on the flat, the rider now seeks continually to improve the suppleness of the horse by riding circles, figures and through turns. This helps to develop the horse's lateral suppleness. In addition, the rider should also be varying the pace by shortening or lengthening the stride, so as to make the horse supple along his length. The ideal is to have a horse that is like a spiral spring which can be compressed, extended or bent easily in either direction.

As the horse becomes more proficient, the ultimate in suppling exercises – the "shoulder-in " must be taught and practiced. This is a classical exercise which horsemen have been using for over 300 years in their training progams and is the movement in which the horse's forehand is bent slightly away from the direction of the movement, so that he moves on two tracks with the forelegs crossing over each other. Once this is mastered, it is relatively easy to teach him to go sideways on the diagonal in the movement called half-pass, in which the hind legs also cross over one another. He must also be taught to turn on the quarters and the forehand – movements in which the forelegs pivot round the hind legs and the hind round the forelegs respectively.

Bottom left: Extended canter with the left foreleg leading.

Left: A nicely balanced canter with the horse moving forward confidently and calmly.

Below: The secondary stage of training improves the balance by riding out across country.

The Pony Club is a nationwide organization which is responsible for training many young riders. Here a lively and alert pony is taken out on morning exercise.

Whatever the style of riding the novice horseman is setting out to master, he has to understand the system of signals (the aids) used to communicate with the horse, and has to learn how to sit so that he can apply these signals most effectively.

An important thing to understand is that it is not possible for a novice rider to learn to ride on a novice horse. Instead, what is needed is a more experienced horse who has already been taught to respond to correctly given aids. Equally essential is a really competent instructor, somebody who understands the anxieties and difficulties a novice rider faces, and who is able to teach him to ride in such a way that it becomes almost second nature.

Because of the importance of the aids in any kind of riding, we will begin by looking at them. They are usually divided into "natural" and "artificial". The natural aids comprise the voice, the legs, the hands and the weight of the rider's body. The artificial aids are whips, spurs and perhaps martingales ("tie-downs" in Western terms), all used to reinforce the action of the natural aids.

In simple terms, the hands control the forehand of the horse (i.e. that part of the horse in front of the saddle) while the legs control the hind part behind the saddle. The legs are used to push the horse forward and to control the position of his quarters and the hands regulate the speed, acting in part as a steering wheel. The body weight is used in a variety of ways. The trunk, although not the seat itself, shifts very slightly to the rear when the rider wants to slow down and the shoulders are also taken back a shade further when the horse is asked to halt. The weight is taken a little forward when the speed increases, and when the rider is sufficiently proficient it can be used very subtly on one side or another in assisting the horse to move sideways.

The voice is a very important aid and one that should be used a lot by horsemen, particularly when schooling young horses. The horse cannot be expected to understand the actual meaning of the words used, but he understands the meaning contained in the tone of the voice and probably, in time, comes to associate a particular set of sounds with a particular request or action. Low, drawn-out and soothing tones act to calm the excitable animal or to reassure a nervous one. A sharp tone of voice will wake up a lazy horse and encourage another to make a greater effort or, used as a growl, can correct or prevent a misdemeanor.

Nonetheless, each individual aid is used only as part of a cohesive system if communication is to be effective, and an understanding of their relationship will help the novice rider to avoid many of the common faults.

Possibly one of the most common of common faults in beginners (who are not absolutely secure in the saddle) is to ride with greater reliance on the hands, or the reins, than is desirable. In fact, horses should be ridden from the back to the front – from the legs into the hands. As we have said, the rider's legs control the hindquarters of the horse, so when they are applied in firm squeezes the effect on a trained horse is to bring the hindlegs further under the body so that they propel him forward with greater energy. In a sense, the quarters are the engine of the horse and the rider's legs act as an accelerator.

The activity generated in the hindquarters by the effective use of the rider's legs is called "impulsion"; once created, the resulting thrust forward has to be controlled by the rider's hands. If the fingers relax and remain open with a light, "give-and-take" contact on the rein, the effect will be an increase of speed as the propulsive power is released. If the fingers close and the rider's legs stop acting, the horse will slow down. If leg pressure is maintained and the fingers of the hand close, the horse's body becomes compressed between the two, so that the stride becomes shorter but very active. If one hand is closed and the other opened while the legs continue to push the horse forward, he will turn to the side on which the hand is closed.

Important though the correct understanding and use of the aids is, they cannot be applied effectively until the rider can sit securely in the saddle, without relying on the reins, and has learned to use hands, legs and body weight without disturbing that security. Early lessons, therefore, should concentrate on positioning the rider "in balance" with the horse and on strengthening his seat.

Below: Trotting on: a group of youngsters being taught in a class lesson in an indoor riding school.

Horses and pupils tend to concentrate better in an enclosed area.

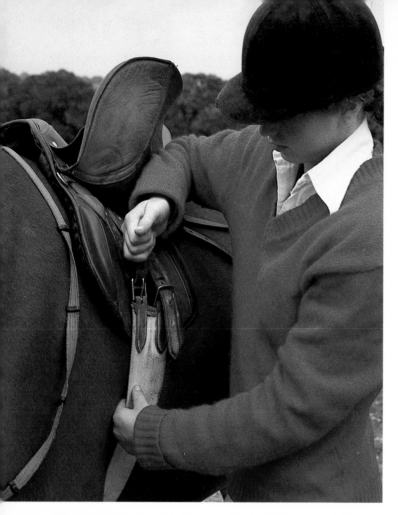

Below: An individual lesson in the indoor school. The school's floor is of shavings, giving a good bouncy surface.

Above: Girthing up the saddle. Initially the girth should not be fastened tightly; it can be adjusted when mounted.

The rider's position

To be "in balance", the rider's weight must be in line with the horse's point of balance, or gravitational center. At rest, standing squarely, the horse's center of balance is at the juncture of an imaginary line drawn from some 6 to 8 in (15 to 20 cm) behind the withers to the ground and a horizontal line drawn from the point of the shoulder to the rear. In movement, the center of balance moves forward in accordance with the speed of the progression – or, when the horse is compressed between leg and hand, it can move slightly to the rear of the stationary point. This happens in the state of "high collection" when the horse, driven forward into a resisting hand, is compressed to an extent where the croup (the highest point of the quarters behind the saddle) is lowered to correspond with the full engagement of the hindlegs under the body, the forehand being raised in consequence. This is the case in the high school movements of *piaffe* and *passage* – piaffe being the elevated trot made virtually on the spot and passage the same trot advancing rhythmically to the front.

Should the weight of the rider be in advance of the horse's center of gravity, at whatever gait, the horse's forehand becomes over-weighted. In consequence the horse is driven downwards into the ground, with a corresponding shortening of the stride. Should the weight be placed behind the center of gravity, the hindquarters, the engine of the horse, are restricted in their movement and there is, again, a loss of freedom in the gaits as well as a loss of forward movement.

The ability of the rider to position his or her weight in accordance with the horse's fluid center of balance at all paces is, therefore, paramount at all times, whatever the style adopted.

The very first lessons of learning to ride are generally concerned with the basic requirements of equitation – the ability to saddle and bridle the horse and to mount and dismount with care. But prior to this most instructors will want their pupils to appreciate the salient points of the rider's seat on the horse, which is actually more easily demonstrated on the ground. The pupil stands with legs apart, hands clasped behind the back, shoulders erect, chest thrown out and head upright, the feet facing directly to the front. The arms are then brought lightly into the sides with the forearms held forward and parallel to the ground. The hands are held upright, the fingers lightly closed with the thumb placed on top. They should be held some 6 in (15 cm) (the width of the bit) apart. The knees are then bent so that shoulders, hips and ankles are in one vertical line. The position is of a person *standing* with his knees bent and not that of someone sitting in a chair, a point to remember when "sitting" in the saddle.

Perhaps the first practical lesson will involve the saddling and bridling of the horse, procedures known as "tacking up". This must be done correctly, to avoid discomfort to either horse or rider.

Tacking up

The saddle is carried to the horse over the forearm with the pommel nearest to the elbow. The stirrup irons will have previously been run up the leathers (on English seat saddles) so that they cannot swing around, and the girth, fastened to the offside girth straps, will be laid over the saddle top. The bridle is carried in the other hand, the reins looped over the headpiece and held at that point. If the saddle has to be put on the ground, it is placed pommel down with the cantle resting against a wall.

The saddle is put on the horse from the near side (left side) and in advance of the withers. It is then slid gently back into place, to lie immediately behind the withers. This way the lie of the hair is not disturbed. The girth is taken down from the seat of the saddle to hang down on the offside, then it is brought under the belly and fastened fairly loosely initially.

The bridle is put on by first slipping the rein over the horse's head, and removing the headcollar or halter if he is wearing one. Both noseband and throatlatch should be unfastened before the bridle is fitted. Standing slightly behind the horse's head, facing the front, the right hand is placed between the ears from behind and holds the bridle by its headpiece. The bit is held flat in the left hand and lifted gently into the mouth, the fingers being used to open the mouth by applying gentle pressure at the sides if necessary. The bridle is then slipped over the ears. The throatlatch is fastened to allow at least three fingers to be inserted between it and the jawbones and the noseband is fastened to fit with room for two fingers.

Left: Putting on the bridle. Right hand encircling the nose, the bit is gently inserted into the mouth with the left hand. Take care not to bang the teeth.

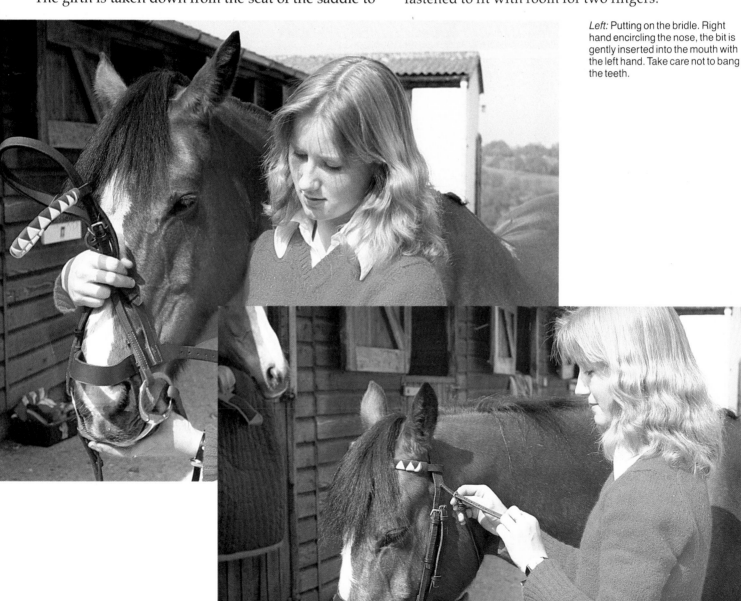

Right: When the bridle is in place the throatlash is fastened. It is important that this should not be fitted too tightly – four fingers should fit easily inside it.

To lead the horse the reins are taken over the head, the rider holding them in the right hand 12 in (80 cm) or so away from the bit and taking the slack across the body to be held in the left hand. To mount, the reins are put back over the horse's head and the girth fastened a hole or two tighter. The rider then positions him or herself at the horse's near-side shoulder facing towards the tail. The reins are picked up in the left hand, any surplus being thrown over the horse's offside shoulder. The near-side rein should be held just slightly shorter than its partner so that should the horse move he is compelled to do so on the arc of a circle *round* the rider and not away from him. The left hand, holding the rein, grasps the pommel, or head, of the saddle.

The rider then takes the near-side stirrup iron and turns the further edge outwards, in a clockwise direction away from the horse's body. The left foot is placed in the iron, the rider takes a couple of hops on the right foot, turning so that the body faces almost broadside to the horse, then the body is pushed up from the ground, the left knee being straightened. The right hand is placed over the center of the saddle,

Anticlockwise from left: To mount, the rider starts by facing the tail. The left foot is put in the iron and the rider springs upward, the right leg swung well clear of the croup. The rider sits gently without startling the horse.

Above right and far right: The "leg-up" is an easier way.

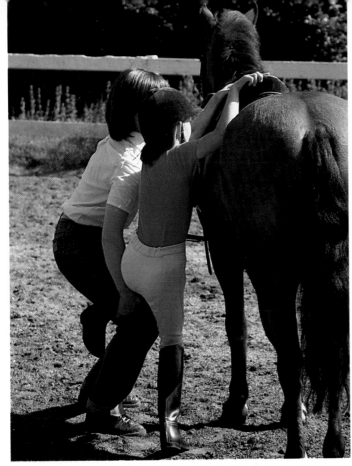

grasping the juncture of the flap with the saddle seat, while almost simultaneously the right leg is swung over the cantle of the saddle. The right leg should be carried over well above the horse's croup, so that there is no danger of him being startled by an inadvertent

blow. Thereafter the rider should lower himself into the saddle as lightly as possible. Bumping down heavily is uncomfortable for the horse; when it happens he will usually react by moving off before his rider is ready for him to do so.

The usual failing is for the novice rider (and sometimes the more experienced rider falls into this trap) to poke the toe of the left foot into the horse's ribs. Not unnaturally he will swing away to avoid the discomfort.

To dismount, both feet should first be taken out of the stirrup irons for reasons of safety. The reins are then held in the left hand and the right one is placed on the pommel. The rider swings the body forward, bringing the right leg over the horse's back, once more ensuring that it does not brush the croup. The landing is made on the balls of the feet, and the knees flexed to absorb the impact.

Once mounted, the leathers need to be checked to see that the length is equal. A guide to the appropriate length is for the ankle to be on a level with the stirrup tread when the foot is taken out of the iron and allowed to hang naturally. To adjust the leathers the foot is kept in the iron (it is both easier and safer) and the leather pulled up or let down as necessary. To check and adjust the girth, the foot is still kept in the iron and one leg (usually the right) moved well forward. The saddle flap can then be lifted and the girth straps pulled up a hole or two.

Below, left to right: Before dismounting, the feet must be taken out of the stirrups. The right leg is swung over the quarters, keeping well clear of the pony, while the left thigh remains in contact with the saddle. Finally the rider touches down, still holding the reins in her left hand.

In the saddle, the pupil should remember the position he tried on the ground; sitting so that there is a straight line between his shoulder, hip and heel. His toes and knees should point to the front, and he should not attempt to grip with his knees since this raises the seat and prevents the rider from sitting deeply in the saddle. It also inhibits the free use of the lower leg. The rein is held inside the little finger of each hand, passing upwards through the palm and secured by the thumb being laid on top. The left thumb points toward the base of the horse's right ear and the right towards the base of the left.

Walk and trot

When the rider can maintain this position at walk, the small of his back being relaxed and following the movement of the pace and his hands following the movement of the mouth (the head and neck which the horse uses as a "balancing pole" is in constant motion at the walk), he can have a go at the rising trot. The trot is a two-time pace, the legs being moved in diagonal pairs (the walk is four-time). A rider may either sit in the saddle or raise his seat slightly out of the saddle for one beat of the pace. This is known as the rising or posting trot.

The actual rising from the saddle should be practiced first at walk; the rider inclines his body slightly forward while keeping his head up and chest open (his shoulders back). The action is really that of

the fork of the body being pushed up to the pommel which will cause the seat bones to rise automatically; it is *not* to push upwards from the knees.

The rising trot is generally quickly mastered by the novice rider, after which he can begin to refine the aids he gives for the movements, concentrating on making them more effective.

The aids for walk from halt are these:

1. The horse is prepared by the rider squeezing momentarily on the girth with both legs while at the same time closing the fingers to obtain contact with the mouth. These actions prepare the horse for the subsequent command.

2. The legs squeeze more decisively and the fingers open to allow the horse to move forward.

To maintain the walk or increase the activity of the pace the legs are applied alternately in little squeezes in tune with the movement.

To go from walk to trot the reins are first shortened a little; the horse is prepared by a quick squeeze of legs and hands acting together; then both legs are applied a little behind the girth and the fingers are opened on the reins. At trot the horse holds his head steady and therefore the rider's hands should be still, maintaining a light contact with the mouth.

To halt or to slow down from trot to walk (the change of pace is called a transition) the horse is prepared similarly, the legs acting first to push him into the hands. The rider's trunk is inclined *very*

Above: The rising trot; the rider rises slightly for one beat of this two-time pace, sitting for one beat.

slightly backwards so that the shoulders are a little behind the hips, the legs remain quietly on the horse's side and the hands act in intermittent squeezes. A rider should never take a dead pull on the reins which would only cause the horse to do exactly the same – pull away in the opposite direction – but with a great deal more strength.

The canter

The canter is perhaps the most pleasant of the paces and is not difficult for a novice once he or she has gained confidence in the feel of the horse at the slower paces. It is a pace of three-time which starts with one or other hindleg, followed by the opposite diagonal pair and finally the other foreleg, which actually appears to be leading the movement. On a right-handed circle the horse should lead with his right or offside foreleg – that is the "inside" foreleg – in order to remain in balance. On a left-handed circle, the near-side foreleg should lead.

The canter is probably best introduced to a novice rider on an uphill slope in company with a steady companion, who will help to ensure that the beginner's horse remains calm and quiet. The object is to give the rider confidence and a feel for the pace, so initially no emphasis needs to be given to the aids or to striking off with one or other foreleg leading. At a canter, the rider inclines his body slightly forward, the inside of his knee and the upper leg remaining in close contact with the saddle and the body anchored by the lowered heel. Providing the rider keeps his loin area supple and follows the movement with an "undulating" motion, there should be no uncomfortable bumping up and down in the saddle.

Once the rider feels relaxed and happy at the canter, he must learn the aids and how to ask the horse to "strike-off" on one leg or the other. The aids for canter on the left lead from trot are these:

1. The rider sits for a few strides instead of rising, preparing the horse by the squeeze of the legs which pushes him onto the hand.

2. He bends the horse very slightly in the required direction (i.e. to the left) by squeezing and raising his left hand. The right hand supports this action by being moved forward a shade. The right leg is applied and held behind the girth (to hold the quarters in place) and the left leg acts firmly on the girth. These aids are transposed for canter on the right-handed circle.

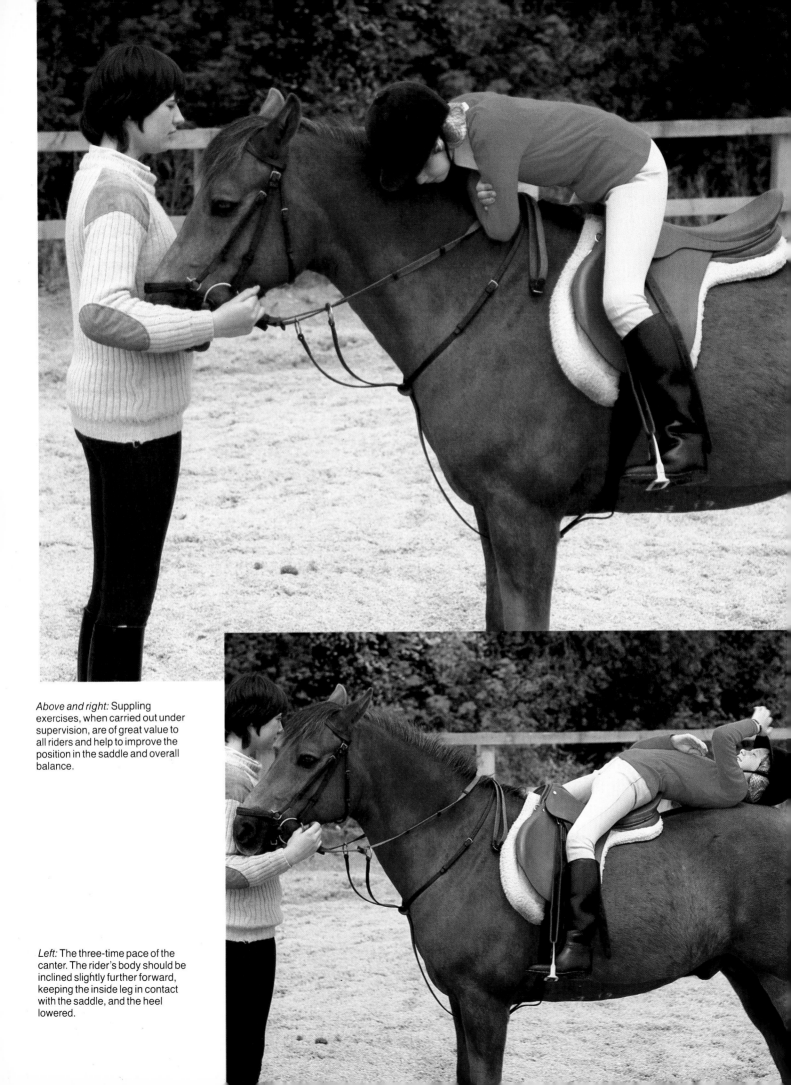

Above and right: Suppling exercises, when carried out under supervision, are of great value to all riders and help to improve the position in the saddle and overall balance.

Left: The three-time pace of the canter. The rider's body should be inclined slightly further forward, keeping the inside leg in contact with the saddle, and the heel lowered.

Exercises

As the rider gains confidence, exercises can be practiced under the supervision of the instructor. These exercises help to supple the body, improve the balance and can be used to correct faults in posture. Initially, they are carried out at halt but thereafter they can be done under the close supervision of the instructor while the horse is walking.

Another exercise for deepening and strengthening the rider's seat is to ride without stirrups for short periods. At a trot, the absence of stirrups makes it less easy to rise and so the rider employs what is called the "sitting trot", in which, as the name suggests, he remains with his seat in contact with the saddle throughout the movement. This is the seat used when schooling (although only for short periods until the horse is well-developed physically and has reached a fairly advanced level of training). It is far easier for the proficient rider to apply the leg aids and those concerned with the disposition of the body weight at a sitting trot than if he is rising at every other stride.

The better the horse is schooled, the more rhythmic the trotting pace will be, and the easier it will also be for the rider to master the sitting trot and be comfortable at this pace. Far more effort is required to sit with ease on a less well-balanced animal.

The rider's back has to be held upright and the upper body must be kept supple through the loins. There is bound to be a jarring effect initially, but if the loins and spine are supple, they should be able to absorb this. The seat should be pushed towards the front of the saddle and the legs seem then to be lifting the horse at each stride. At no time should the rider be pushing downwards with the seat – such movement as there is must always be upwards and forwards.

Without any doubt at all the exercise which establishes a deep secure seat, improves the balance immeasurably and gives a feel for the movement of the horse, is that which works the rider, without stirrups, on the lunge. It is this form of instruction that will really benefit the rider, helping him to become an educated, all-round horseman.

It requires, however, a very experienced instructor in combination with a horse well accustomed to the work and with easy paces. A variety of exercises at walk, trot and canter are employed. In an ideal world (such as the classical schools), one would consider a program extending over a full twelve months – four months to work on stabilizing the rider's balance, four to obtain ease and absolute freedom of the body posture and four to establish and develop the strength of the seat.

Above right: When riding uphill, the rider's body has to be inclined forward to assist the horse by ensuring the rider's weight does not restrict the quarters.

Right: This exercise, carried out on both sides, supples the rider's waist and the small of the back, and improves her balance and confidence.

Far right: A good basic position is important. The rider should sit deep in the saddle, with an upright but balanced and relaxed posture.

Left: The sitting trot. Here the rider sits in the saddle without rising, letting her back swing with the movement of the horse's back, helping to create impulsion.

This series of pictures shows the exercise which is called "Round the World". The rider turns through 360° in the saddle. It helps the rider to be supple and feel confident, but it is important that it is done only under supervision.

Learning to jump

Jumping a horse, an essential element in English seat riding, is no more difficult to master than the rising or sitting trot, or the canter. Once the rider is able to ride "in balance" on the flat and exert an acceptable degree of control over the horse, he will find jumping presents few problems.

Training the rider to jump – as with training the young horse – begins with walking and trotting over a grid of heavy poles laid on the ground, spaced between 4 to 6 ft (1.2 to 1.8 m) apart, according to the length of stride of the horse. The rider should incline his trunk slightly forward and use his legs against the horse's sides in time with the movement. His hands should move forward to follow the horse's lowered head as he first walks and then trots briskly over the poles. Mastering this exercise could be termed mastering the "ABC" of jumping and once perfected, it makes the next steps easy to accomplish.

The follow-up to the ground grid exercise is the succession of cavalletti arranged first at their lowest height of 10 in (25 cm) and then raised to 15 in (38 cm). After this, in a row of, say, five cavalletti, number four is moved up to number five so that a little spread fence is produced. The horse should still be asked to trot over the cavalletti, this being good for the balance of both horse and rider. It may be, however, that the rider's shoulders, elbows and hands have to move forward a shade further as the horse takes this little obstacle, in order for the rider to remain in balance and allow the horse to extend his neck still more.

The next step is to make a slightly bigger fence by placing number four cavalletto on top of number five to make a sloped (staircase type) fence of about 2 ft (60 cm) in height. It is now advisable for the rider to shorten the leathers by a hole or two, so as to be able to put more weight on the knee and thigh and so that the angle between his trunk and thigh can be closed more than previously at the moment of take-off. The seat is then raised a little from the saddle, the shoulders lead the movement forward and are followed by the elbow and hand. The leg should be used more strongly than previously, following the crossing of the last grid cavalletto prior to the small jump. If the shoulders are straightened a little on landing, the seat will be touching the saddle automatically as the jump is completed.

Below: A cavalletti grid placed at its lowest level is a good introduction to jumping for both horse and rider.

Next, a fence should be placed 20 ft (6 m) or so from the grid, to be jumped from canter, although the grid itself is still crossed at a trot. So long as the rider is ready to move forward as the horse prepares to take-off he will not be "left behind" by the movement.

The next stage is to remove the guideline of the poles or grid. However, so as to help the rider to gauge the take-off stride correctly a "distance" pole or cavalletto should be placed 20 to 22 ft (6 to 6.5 m) in front of a small fence of sloping poles, built no more than about 2 ft (60 cm) in height but as firm and solid as possible. This allows one non-jumping canter stride between the two obstacles. The rider, having approached in canter, must apply the legs once on landing over the cavalletto and once more, with greater emphasis, for the actual take-off.

If this is then followed by a further fence 33 ft (10 m) away – after two non-jumping strides – it will mean that the rider must continue to apply leg pressure after landing from the center jump in order to prepare the horse for the final obstacle. This teaches the rider to estimate or "to see the stride" and, with practice, should have no difficulty in presenting the horse to arrive correctly at the take-off point of any obstacle.

Thereafter the rider needs to school over an increasing variety of fences of every type possible: parallels, uprights, staircases and pyramids, and to begin riding over small courses involving changes of direction. He should also be riding out over open country, particularly over terrain where he will encounter both upward and downward slopes. In both instances, the rider should incline the trunk forward so as to allow the horse the freedom of his quarters.

In the schooling session, in the menage, another important movement – the rein-back – must be mastered, again with the help of an instructor. The rider has to ride the horse energetically into halt, ensuring, by the strong action of the legs, that the horse halts with his quarters engaged under his body and with his head lowered. The rider must then lighten his seat by inclining his trunk just a shade forward, while applying his legs to push the horse up into his hands, which close and obstruct the forward movement. Placed in such a position, the horse, helped by tactful indications made by the hands, must then move backwards, and he should do this in two-time, moving the legs in diagonal pairs.

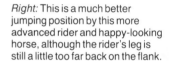

Right: This is a much better jumping position by this more advanced rider and happy-looking horse, although the rider's leg is still a little too far back on the flank.

Left: The rider is not interfering with the horse's mouth, but her seat is too far out of the saddle, her body leaning too far forward and her leg away from the saddle.

Horse and rider in Western tack.
Palominos are frequently used for
Westen riding.

Right: Calf-roping is a popular
Western activity which has highly
practical uses.

Western riding and equipment

Western horsemanship has its origins in the "other school of riding" which was brought to perfection in the Iberian Peninsula and came to America with the sixteenth-century Spanish conquistadores. Even in this day of turbo jets and microchips, cowboys and many thousands of leisure riders still throw the same saddles over their horses' backs as their forebears did 100 years ago and still value the same loyalty, obedience and a "quick turn of hoof" in their mounts.

The Western style of riding is as familiar to riders west of the Mississippi and south of the Mason-Dixon Line as the English seat is to the "hunting and jumping" fraternity. Throughout vast areas of North and South America, Western saddles are the only kind ever used at home or in the riding school; horse shows and rodeos are filled with classes for the Western-trained horse and rider and magazines with titles like *Western Horseman* are devoted to their needs.

A look at the history of the western states and Canada explains why a style of riding so very different from that imported into the New World by the first English Colonials developed. To begin with, as we know, the first explorers to make any impact in the west were Spanish. Spanish saddles had high pommels and cantles and were, in keeping with the Spanish love of gold, silver, jewelry and other adornments, highly decorated. Bridles were either hackamores (bitless) or featured the very severe spade bit, known for its long cheeks or shanks (the part of the bit seen on the sides of the horse's mouth), and high port (the hump in the middle of the bit) which could dig into the roof of the horse's mouth. Even the terminology used today in this style of riding stems from those Spanish beginnings: cinch, or girth, comes from *cinchas; lariat* still means the cowboy's rope.

Above: A Western saddle. The wide stirrup leathers keep the rider's leg away from the horse's sweating flanks.

Spanish influence

These Spanish equipment imports formed the basis for Western riding, just as their Barb and Arab horses became the foundation stock for herds of roaming Mustangs, not only because it was the only gear ever seen by many western inhabitants, both Indian and white, but because it provided the only logical solution to the problem of sore backs (horses') and stiff muscles (riders') caused by long hours in the saddle. High cantles and pommels also provided security, especially for "beginners" who had no recourse to riding lessons, but were simply expected to get into the saddle and stay there all day.

The modern version of the Western saddle, although refined over the last century or two, retains many of the basic features which the Spanish extolled. The pommel and cantle are lower, but still high enough to offer support and safety to the rider. The long wide skirts (the side flaps) spread the rider's weight over a large area of the horse's back so that, even though the saddle may weigh 40 pounds (18 kilograms), the horse will still be full of energy after a 100 mile (160 kilometer) ride. Wide stirrup leathers are designed to keep the rider's legs away from the horse's sweating flanks.

The hardwood stirrups are better than metal, which is hot in summer and cold in winter, and, if enclosed in a box or *tapadero*, protect the rider's foot from thorns. The lack of padding under the saddle eliminates potential lumps caused by the horse's sweating in extreme heat –but is compensated for by the use of one or more blankets, which also enables any saddle to be used on virtually any horse.

One major refinement is the elimination of a sloping seat (the part of the saddle the rider sits on), which used to throw the rider's legs forward and his weight to the rear. The stirrup leathers have been moved to the middle of the saddle in keeping with this, thus allowing the rider to sit over the horse's center of gravity, with his leg slightly bent at the knee, maintaining a straight line from heel to hip. This position – which is, in fact, almost exactly the same as the classical European riding position – ensures better balance of both horse and rider.

Other refinements are the development of the "horn" – the large bump on the front of the saddle – intended to hold the lariat, and the addition of a second cinch added towards the rear of the saddle which, while kept fairly slack, comes into play during calf-roping, preventing the extra pressure on the horn pulling the saddle up and forward.

Bridles, too, were altered, with bits becoming milder, although still generally containing a higher port and longer shanks than their English counterparts, in order to ensure instant response to a cowboy whose life could depend on quick reactions. Hackamores became known as bosals, with control coming from the heavy noseband that puts pressure on the horse's sensitive nasal bones.

Left: A Western bridle with the very severe spade bit. This has a high "port" or hump in the middle which can dig into the roof of the horse's mouth. Note the long cheeks.

Below: Western riders hold both reins in one hand and steer the horse by neck reining, pulling the reins to the side of the neck opposite the direction wanted.

Chaps and bandannas

Clothing developed out of the same practicality which influenced the tack. Leather chaps protect the rider's leg and his trousers; a wide-brimmed hat protects his head from both sun and rain, and may also be used – in extremis – to water and feed his horse; a bandanna worn round his neck doubles as a sweat rug, towel, dust mask and, if necessary, bandage; high boots offer foot protection and high heels prevent the foot slipping through the stirrup and allow the cowboy to "dig his heels in" when roping; the spurs originally jingled so that a horse would, theoretically at least, know when his rider was coming. Contrary to much popular thought, there is no part of a working Western rider's clothing that was designed purely for "show".

Good Western riders use the same aids and, as already indicated, sit in a more or less similar position to the English horseman. The major difference between the two styles of riding can be seen in the method of holding the reins. Western riders hold both reins in one hand, whereas English riders use two hands. Steering the Western horse is done by neck reining: if the rider wants to turn left, he moves his hands slightly to the right, and the touch of the reins on the left side of the horse's neck provides the indication that he is to move in that direction. Obviously the Western horse is taught to recognize and respond to this signal in his early training.

Two distinct styles of Western riding have developed, however: Californian and Texan. Californian horsemen have a stronger contact, and the horses a more collected way of going with shorter, bouncier strides. They also tie their reins together, whereas Texans leave them split, so that when they dismount, the reins drop to the ground, providing a sign to the horse that he is to stand still.

A Western-trained horse moves in an easier, looser, generally more "laid-back" way than English horses, and a good horse will change his paces, or way of going, according to his tack. He is still expected to give a balanced, controlled and comfortable ride, though, and certain movements used in Western riding, such as the flying change (when a horse changes leading leg at every stride of canter), are similar to those practiced by dressage riders.

Emergency stop

Some movements are peculiar to the Western horse, however. These include the quick stop and, even faster, the sliding stop, in which the horse's hind legs slide underneath him to enable him to stop almost instantly, lifting his forelegs off the ground slightly in the process.

Quick stops, sliding stops and pivots, in which the horse pivots around on his hind legs, the forelegs coming slightly off the ground, are all part of the horse's daily life of working cattle, and thus are asked for in Western horse shows. Complete obedience, as seen in the trail class in which horses are asked to

Above: Doing up the cinch on a Western saddle. Note the thick blanket worn under the saddle which enables any saddle to be used on almost any horse and also doubles as a blanket.

negotiate various often strange obstacles, speed and quick turns, such as those demonstrated in barrel racing and roping, and smooth balanced paces are all required of the well-trained Western horse. Good horsemanship is no less prized, and rough hands, an unbalanced seat and similar faults are condemned by all serious Western horsemen.

In the final analysis, riding – whether English seat or Western – is a universal skill, depending upon general principles which are commonly held. The differences are concerned with matters of detail and, to some extent, with the uses to which the horse is put.

New Forest ponies in good condition in the wild.

Most "ordinary" horses and ponies are happier and healthier living out at grass provided certain requirements are met. The exceptions are the most highly-bred animals – those that contain a high proportion of Thoroughbred or Arabian blood, or those whose owners require them to be kept at the peak of fitness. It is less time consuming to keep an animal at grass, and a lot easier on the purse strings.

Those people who have time to ride only on weekends should consider that keeping an animal at grass ensures that at least he receives adequate exercise during weekdays but it does not, of course, absolve the owner of all responsibility from Monday to Friday. Although grass is the horse's natural food, when in the wild he is free to roam at will over wide areas in his search for it and can pick and choose the most nutritious offerings. In the domesticated state the horse is confined to a paddock and so has to rely on his owner to provide him with the nutrients unavailable in his relatively small grazing area. He also needs a daily check to make sure he is in good health and has sustained no injury as he wanders around his paddock.

The minimum amount of grass required for one small horse is one acre (0.4 hectare), and double this amount is preferable. The smaller the area, the more careful must be its management, and the more supplementary feed a horse will need. A horse will not thrive on scrubby or poor pasture; fertilizers and lime will need to be applied to the pasture regularly, proportions and type being determined by soil analysis. Horses are epicurean grazers and will leave any areas of weed and rank grass, so it is a good idea to alternate the grazing of horses with that of other livestock such as cattle or sheep if at all possible. This will also help to reduce worm parasites since those affecting horses do not have the same adverse effect on ruminants.

Great care should be taken to ensure that there are no poisonous plants in the paddock. Ragwort, yew, foxglove, hemlock, laburnum, laurel, ivy, privet, belladonna (deadly nightshade) and rhododendron (to name but a few) are all poisonous, and if eaten in sufficient quantities any of these could prove fatal.

Fencing

The best form of fencing for horses is post-and-rails, but this is also the most expensive and provides no shelter from the prevailing winds. Hedges offer protection, but, if they are to be effective, they must be strong and stout, free from poisonous plants and gaps. Ponies in particular have an infuriating habit of being able to creep through the smallest space. The fencing most commonly used is wire and this, provided it is of the plain, heavy gauge variety strung tightly between solid wooden posts, is quite satisfactory. The bottom line should be strung at least 1 ft (30 cm) from the ground so that a horse cannot get his front feet caught in it, and there should be at least two lines of wire above this one. Barbed wire should never be used as it can cause terrible injuries.

Electric fencing may be used in order to "strip-graze" a piece of land; after the initial (harmless) shock, horses will not go near it again. A strand of electric fencing may also be put along the top of post-and-rail fencing to discourage horses from leaning on the fence and breaking the rails. Fencing should be inspected daily for broken wire, broken rails, or gaps in hedges.

Gates are equally important; strong wooden or metal ones which swing easily on the hinges are the best and there are a number of acceptable safety fastenings on the market. If the field is any distance from the house it is advisable to fit a padlock and chain to the supporting posts around both the opening and hinged ends, especially in town and urban areas where horse-rustling is by no means uncommon.

In this connection, too, it is worth thinking about the painless operation of freeze-branding your horse. Organizations in several countries operate a register of all horses who have been freeze-marked, and in addition to more rapid tracing, it has been shown to reduce the incidence of thieving. A freeze marker is applied to the horse's back, killing the pigmented hair and leaving a bald area which re-grows white hair in a sequence of letters and numbers within a few weeks.

Above: Never use barbed wire for fencing. When it is slack like this, horses can easily get caught up in it and hurt.

Below: A freeze-marking register now operates in some countries and makes lost or stolen ponies easier to trace.

Above: This wooden field shelter gives much-needed protection for the horse at grass from flies in summer and from wind, rain and snow during the winter months.

Shelter

If no hedges are available for protection, a field shelter must be provided. Even though a number of horses will appear to ignore it at first, it does provide protection from driving wind and rain and, equally important, from the worst of the flies in summer. It should be open on one side and sufficiently large to shelter several horses if they are to be turned out together. It provides a dry place in which to feed, and, for those owners who have no stabling facilities, it also provides somewhere to groom and tack up before a ride.

It is a good idea to have a hay rack fitted on the inner long side of the shelter where hay can be fed in the winter, and a ring should be fitted fairly high up, to provide somewhere to tie the animals for grooming. This ring can also be used to secure a haynet if no hayrack is fitted. Some horses delight in chewing fences, trees and the like – often, but not always, because they are short of minerals. A mineral (salt) lick fixed in the shelter out of the rain will usually cure this. A constant supply of fresh water must be available, the best method being to have a piped connection to a trough, with the supply automatically regulated. Any large, free standing container may be used to provide water, but it should have no sharp edges or protuberances on which the horse could damage himself. If the field contains a spring this can be used to advantage and usually has the benefit of not becoming frozen in the winter. However, if it is very shallow, the horse may pick up small particles of sand or dirt as he drinks and this can cause colic. A stagnant pond should be fenced off from use. Remember that ice will probably have to be broken on a container of water most days during the winter.

In winter there is little or no growth of grass, and that which there is contains no goodness, so hay will have to be supplied in quantity, plus a ration of hard concentrate feed to keep a horse warm, as well as appeasing his appetite. The amount will depend on the amount of work the animal is expected to do, but a feed of nuts, bran and perhaps sugar beet or barley will be appreciated and is a necessity if the weather is particularly bad.

The horse should be wormed every six to eight weeks to prevent worm infestation. This is particularly important on small acreages.

If the horse is expected to do any concentrated work during the winter, an occasional day's hunting or a jumping event perhaps, it may be advisable to clip him partially; this makes it easier to condition him as he will not sweat up so easily. If he has been clipped it will be necessary to provide him with a New Zealand rug, which should be checked at least once, and preferably twice, a day to make sure it is not rubbing, and to adjust it if it has slipped to one side during rolling.

In any case the horse must be visited daily both in summer and winter, regardless of whether or not he is being ridden or in receipt of feed, and checked over for any scratches, knocks or kicks, and to pick out his feet.

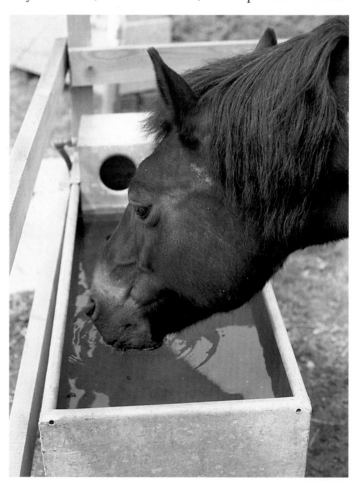

Above: A constant supply of fresh water must be available. This piped supply to an outdoor trough is ideal.

Right: Trees also provide shade in summer and a certain amount of shelter from the elements in winter.

If your horse is more highly-bred or in regular work he will need to be kept stabled, or on the "combined" system, when the horse is kept stabled at night and allowed to run out in the paddock during the day in winter, and vice versa in summer, when he will appreciate being kept away from irritating flies. It also combats the boredom of being confined to his stable for all but two or three hours of the day, gives him time to relax and unwind, and provides exercise if for some reason you are unable to ride every day.

Before embarking on keeping a stabled horse, you must understand that it is a very time-consuming occupation; the never-ending routine of feeding, watering, mucking-out, grooming, exercising, bedding down and feeding again, must be carried out daily, year in, year out.

The stable

Most stable complexes today consist of a pre-fabricated wooden loose box, either in singles, or several attached in a row, with a tack room and feed shed. These pre-fabricated buildings are perfectly acceptable provided they are lined for warmth and strength, and are sited sensibly on a gently sloping concrete base.

In many parts of Europe and the United States, individual stable boxes are built inside a large barn, rows of boxes on each side being divided by a passageway down the center and with sliding main doors for entrance and exit at each end. This system has many advantages especially in adverse weather conditions when all stable chores can be completed in the dry.

If erecting your own stable, position it so that it faces south if possible, away from the colder winds and in a position that will enable the always-inquisitive horse to see as much as possible of what is going on around him. This will help to alleviate boredom. Ideally, the box should be about 14 ft x 12 ft (4.2 m x 3.6 m) for a horse, and 12 ft x 12 ft (3.6 m x 3.6 m) for a pony, so that the animal can move around easily and will not get "cast" when he lies down. It should be of sufficient height for the air to circulate freely and to prevent him from banging his head on the roof.

The door should be wide enough to prevent him from knocking a hip against it when entering or leaving the box, and of sufficient height to prevent him from jumping out over it, while being low enough for him to look out. A half-door is traditionally the best with the top part of the door left open to provide light and a free flow of air. The window should be positioned on the same side as the door, and should open inwards, the glass protected on the inside by bars or wire mesh. Door fastenings should be secure with bolts top and bottom, or a kick-over fastening at the bottom and a bolt at the top.

The roof should be pitched downwards towards the door so that the rain runs off easily with an overlap over the door to create a canopy. Light switches are fitted outside the stable where a horse cannot reach them.

The stable needs to be fitted with a manger; triangular ones made of heavy plastic and fitting into a bar placed across the corner of the box are ideal as they can be removed easily for regular cleaning. A ring should be secured to the wall fairly high up to which the horse can be tied for grooming, tacking up and so on, and provided it is high enough it can also be used for tying up the haynet if a hay rack is not used. This latter is a metal grid usually placed across a corner of the box into which the hay is put, and is useful if the horse is a confirmed haynet eater.

Above: This loose box door is just the right height for this pony to see over. Each door must have top and bottom bolts.

Clean water must be available at all times and can be supplied in heavy duty plastic or rubber buckets. If the horse is prone to kicking them over, a piece of wood fastened across the corner of the box into which the bucket can be slotted will prevent this happening. An expensive, but very successful, alternative is an automatic self-filling water bowl. All water containers and feed containers should be scrubbed out regularly.

Having sited the stable, you must then consider the positioning of the feed room, hay store, tack room, muck heap, and water supply, all of which should be near at hand. Feed, hay and bedding must be stored under cover, the former in vermin-proof containers. Hay and straw should preferably be stored slightly above ground level.

Left: A row of loose boxes facing onto the yard where the inhabitants can watch what is going on around them.

Below: A metal hay rack is useful for haynet eaters!
Below right: A metal holder keeps the water bucket upright.

Bedding

Wheat straw is the most widely used form of bedding in regions where it is available: horses tend to eat oat and barley straw. Wood shavings, sawdust, peat, shredded or diced paper (a fairly recent innovation) are all satisfactory, paper particularly so if the horse is prone to dust allergies. However, both peat and sawdust tend to heat up when wet, so it is important to remove soiled patches regularly and also to pick the horse's feet out several times a day to remove tightly packed bedding. Whatever the bedding, it must be spread deep to encourage the horse to lie on it, and prevent him injuring himself when he does so – and it should be banked up around the sides of the stable to keep out the drafts and to prevent injury should he get cast.

Ideally, the stable should be mucked out (cleaned out) every day, droppings and wet straw taken to the muck heap, the floor swept, and the rest of the straw shaken down again, together with some clean. A satisfactory alternative, the deep litter system, involves just picking up the droppings and the very worst of the soiled bedding every day and adding clean bedding on top, saving working time until the stable is mucked out thoroughly once a week.

Routine

Daily routine begins with the horse's breakfast, the amount required naturally depending on his build and work. Once his water bucket has been refilled and rugs (if he is wearing them) straightened, he should be checked over for possible overnight damage before being left in peace to digest his meal. Mucking out follows, and a quick brush over before being exercised or turned out in the paddock. Back from exercise the horse will need a thorough grooming, as the grease will have been brought to the surface of his coat. Replace his rugs and give him a small haynet or feed if he is in hard work, and then leave him until his evening feed.

If he has been turned out for the day, the horse should be brought in in the early evening, brushed and checked over before being given his evening feed. The largest portion of a stabled horse's hay should be given as late as is practicable in the evening, and his water bucket refilled.

Below left: Horses are not always bedded on straw. Shredded paper may be used, or this horse looking out of his loose box has a bed of wood shavings.

Below: The bed should be deep enough to encourage the horse to lie down, and banked at the sides to prevent possible injury. The stable should be mucked out every day.

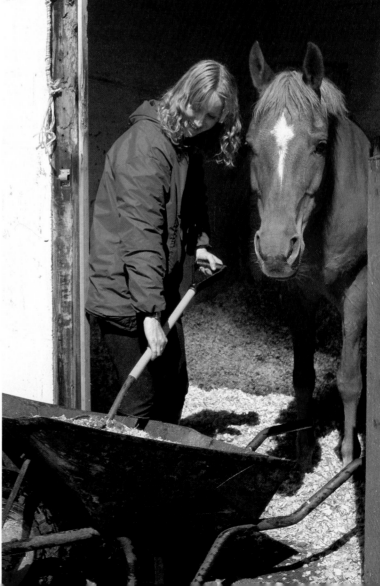

Right: Mucking out. This is one of the stable chores that has to be carried out daily. Droppings and wet straw are removed and taken to the muck heap, the floor swept and new straw added to make a good deep bed of clean straw.

Below: The horse will not thrive in muddy conditions like this. With no grass he will need supplementary feeding and a good supply of hay.

Grooming and Clipping

The stabled horse must be groomed regularly to keep his coat and skin healthy, and to prevent disease, as well as to improve his appearance. The grass-kept horse needs to keep a degree of grease (which can be removed with thorough brushing) in his coat to keep him warm, but the stabled horse is not so dependent on the elements, and in cold weather will usually wear a rug to keep his temperature constant.

Left: A well-shod hoof. When picking out the feet, the hoof pick should be drawn down away from the heel towards the point of the frog, removing all dried mud and stones.

Below left: The body brush is used with the lie of the coat to remove grease and scurf . . .
Below: . . . and to brush out the tangles from the tail, a few hairs at a time.

Grooming should be a strenuous exercise: a daily "lick-and-a-promise" is of no benefit at all. Start by cleaning out feet, picking up each in turn and drawing the hoof pick down either side of the frog to remove anything – dried mud or stones – that may have lodged there. At the same time check the shoes for looseness, wear or movement, and the clenches to ensure they have not risen. Remove any dried mud or stubborn sweat stains from the coat and legs with the dandy brush: this brush should never be used on the head. Take the opportunity while brushing the legs to feel for any lumps, cuts or swellings and deal with them accordingly.

The body brush and curry comb are next used together, one in each hand, the brush being used firmly along the coat to remove the grease and to promote circulation. The brush should be scraped over the teeth of the curry comb to remove the dirt that accumulates in it from the coat. The body brush is used to clean the head, but care must be taken not to bang the eyes and nose, which are obviously sensitive. The body brush should also be used to brush the mane and tail, releasing and brushing just a few hairs at a time from the tail. The eyes and nose should then be sponged with one damp sponge and the dock with the other.

Finally, the stable rubbing pad or wisp is used on the neck, shoulders and quarters only. This should be brought down forcefully on these areas (never on the ribs or bony regions) to tone up the muscles and promote circulation, before giving a final wipe over to shine up the coat. If necessary the mane and tail can be laid with a damp water brush. The hooves can then be oiled and the tail bandaged; before bandaging dampen the top of the tail but never the bandage, which would tighten on the dock as it dried, causing discomfort.

Above: It is vital to wash the mane and tail periodically, using a mild shampoo, to keep the hair clean and to make sure the horse looks really smart before showing.

If you intend to do a lot of work with the horse during the winter months, it will probably be necessary to clip him in order to keep him in condition, enabling him to do harder work without sweating up so much. There are several types of clip; the full clip, when the hair is completely removed from all parts of the body; the hunter clip, in which the hair is removed except for a saddle patch and the hair on the legs; and the trace clip, which entails removing the hair from the belly, the underside of the neck, between the thighs and across the chest. Some people will also remove the hair from the head and neck, which is called a blanket clip. Both the blanket and the trace clip are frequently used on horses kept on the "combined system" or those living out (they must, however, wear a New Zealand rug).

Clipping should not take place until the winter coat has grown right through, usually in the fall, and the horse will probably need to be clipped again after Christmas. Once clipped, he will need to wear a rug (or rugs) in the stable. If he is turned out during the day he will need to wear a New Zealand rug.

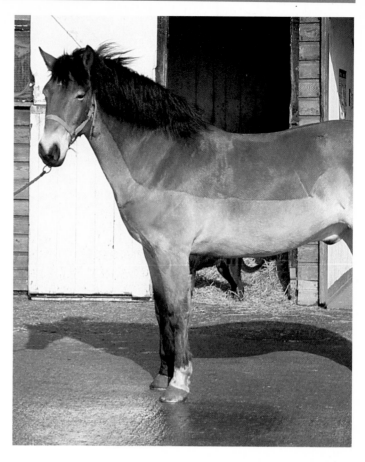

Below: A rubber or plastic curry comb is useful to remove the old coat when the pony is molting and to remove caked mud from a pony who is living out at grass.

Right: A trace clip is often seen on ponies working during the winter.
Below right: Even if the shoes are not worn, the feet grow and the horn must be pared.

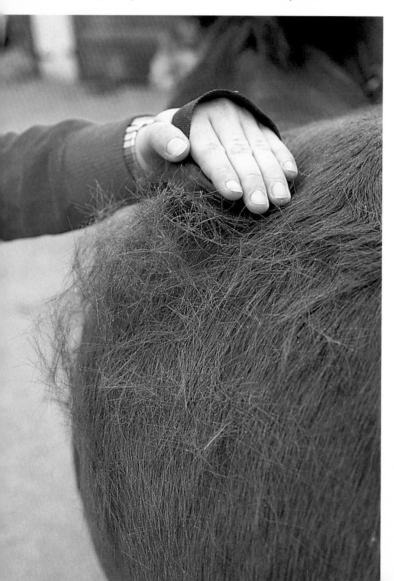

Shoeing

Feet will need regular attention from the farrier approximately every six to eight weeks. Even if the shoes are not worn down or loose, the horn will have grown, pushing the shoes in at the heel. They will therefore need removing so that the hooves can be rasped down before the shoes are refitted. Quite probably, however, the clenches will have risen and the shoes become loose in consequence or have worn thin. Shoes can be applied by a hot or cold method, the former generally more satisfactory since a better fit can be obtained.

The horse must have his feet attended to by a farrier about every six to eight weeks. A better fitting can be obtained if the horse is hot-shod, but this is less usual nowadays.

Feeding

A correct balance and quantity of food is essential to overall health, for the maintenance of body temperature, the replacement of tissue wastage, the build-up and maintenance of body condition and the supply of energy required for movement.

If the horse is to work satisfactorily he must be fed a ration of energy-producing protein, and the amount of energy feed he receives must bear a direct relationship to the amount of energy he expends. A horse living out and doing very little or no work can exist completely off good grass in summer, with the addition of hay and a little food in winter, but the stabled horse in work should receive food containing protein, bulk fiber, fats, starches, salts and vitamins. These are contained to a greater or lesser degree in oats, maize and barley which are high in starch and fat. Bulk food is provided by grass and hay, bran, sugar beet pulp and carrots; salts are present in hay, and necessary vitamins in small quantities in all foods.

The horse's temperament plays a large part when considering what food he should receive. Some horses "jump out of their skin" on a handful of oats and others need large quantities of it before they have the energy to perform even light work. It is not possible to advise on quantities as it varies greatly according to the horse and conditions. The only rough guide is the condition and obesity (or lack of it) of the individual animal. In the main, horses being worked every day should receive equal parts of bulk and concentrate foods; the more work they do the more concentrates they need. Bulk food should never fall below one-third of the total amount of food received, but it should be stressed, however, that all horses are individuals, and should be treated as such, particularly over the delicate task of feeding.

Above: The dull, staring coat and prominent ribs and hips denote that this horse is in poor condition. A horse needs enough and the right kind of food to maintain peak condition.

Right: The same horse as shown above photographed some six months later. Note how proper care and feeding have resulted in greatly improved condition.

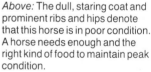

Left: When feeding hay in a net, ensure that the net is tied securely and sufficiently high up to prevent the horse from pawing it and getting his feet caught up in it.

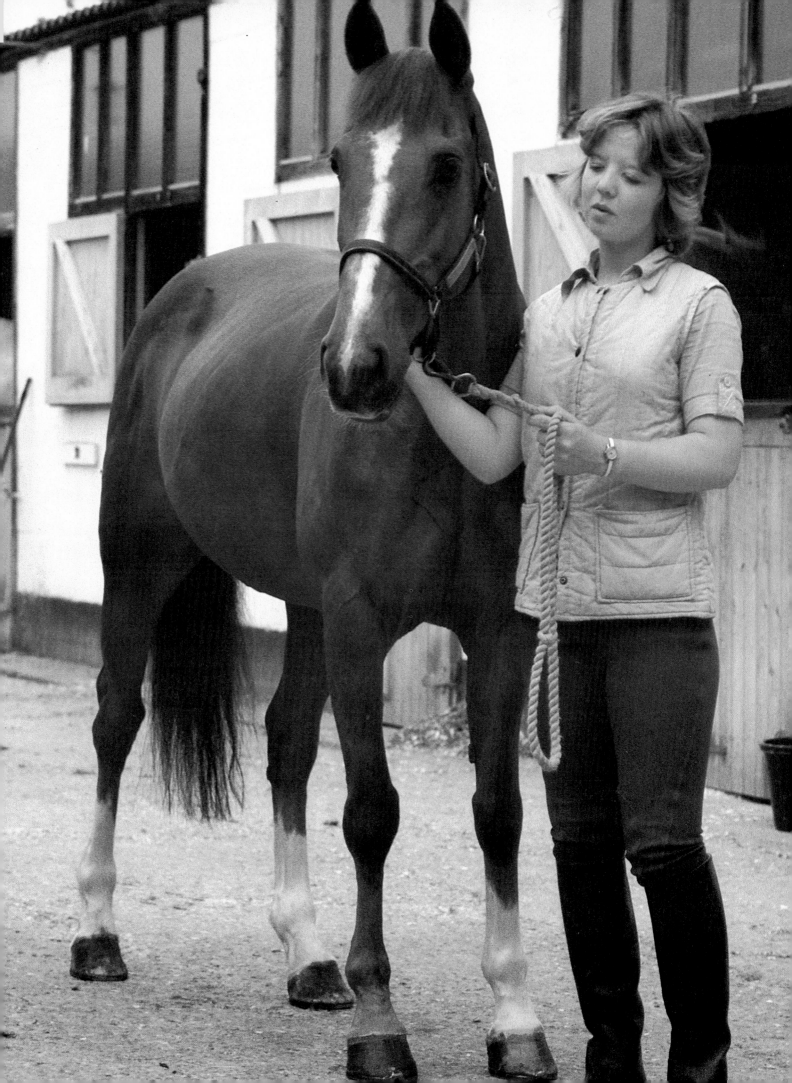

A clear indication of a horse in good condition is his bright eye and general alert and inquisitive appearance. An ailing horse tends to be dull and unresponsive.

A healthy and happy horse will perform better and respond to his rider's wishes more readily than one with even a small ailment or one that is suffering from neglect. A fit horse, free from pain or irritation, will tell the world he is in fine form by carrying his head proudly and pricking his ears back and forth. He will look alert and interested in his surroundings and his innocent curiosity about anything new that comes within his view will be evident.

It is essential for the horse owner to be able to recognize whether or not his horse is in good health, and to be able to treat simple injuries and ailments. However, it is equally important to know when to call the veterinarian; unskilled treatment can be dangerous to the horse.

GENERAL SIGNS OF HEALTH AND DISEASE

To recognize when the horse is off-color or in pain, it is necessary first to know the signs and appearance of a normal, healthy horse.

The first obvious sign of good health is a coat which lies flat and has a gloss on it, although this is naturally more noticeable in a stabled horse than in one living out-of-doors. If the hairs of the coat are more upright - a "staring" coat – and if it looks dull and lifeless, the indication is that all is not well. Such signs can indicate worm or lice infestation or even malnutrition. The ribs and hindquarters should be well-covered and rounded.

The eyes should be clear and bright and the surrounding membranes, together with those of the nostrils, should be a healthy-looking pink color as opposed to red or yellow – possible indications of inflammation or jaundice.

A healthy horse should stand squarely on all four feet. Resting a hindleg is quite normal, provided he is not always resting it, which may indicate pain in that leg. Resting a foreleg is not so common and should be investigated. All legs should be cool to the touch and free from any swellings. Heat and puffiness are sure indications of strains and sprains. Make a daily habit of running your hands down your horse's legs so that you know instantly if any new lumps or bumps develop.

Droppings and urine are good indications of the horse's health. Droppings should be well formed (although they may vary slightly in color and consistency) passed regularly and frequently and free from strong odor, and urine should be virtually colorless.

If a horse rejects his food, or drops balls of it when eating, it may be a sign that his teeth are in need of attention. Call the veterinary surgeon to rasp any sharp edges.

Below: The sheen of the coat and the well-covered ribs and hindquarters show that this horse is in fine condition.

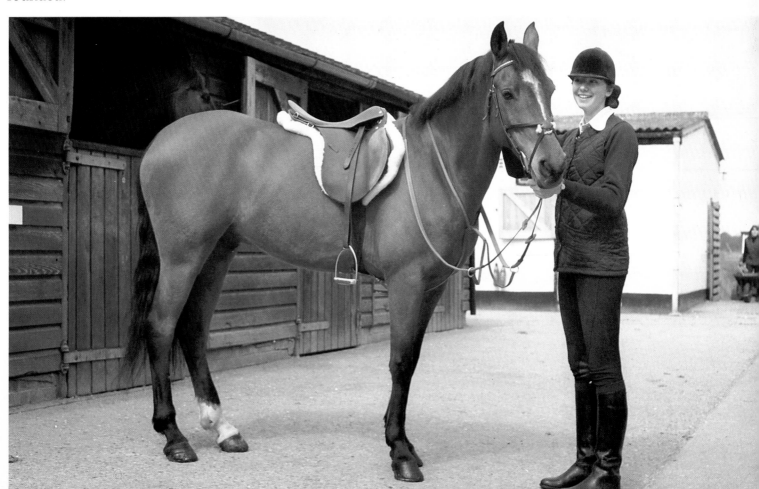

Behavior

A horse who is feeling unwell will probably change his behavior somewhat. A quiet, easily-handled horse may become nervous, while a nervous, excitable one could turn quiet and cooperative. It is important, therefore, that you know your horse's normal behavior pattern. If he looks dull and lifeless, lies down more frequently than usual and remains so even when you enter the stable, something is wrong.

Temperature, pulse and respiration

The horse's normal temperature is between 100°F and 101.5°F; anything much over this points to a fever. You should, however, know exactly what your own horse's normal temperature is as it varies slightly from one animal to another. Take his temperature and record it when he is healthy (but not when he is excited as his temperature will rise).

The normal pulse rate is between 35 and 40 beats per minute, although after lively exercise this may be as high as 100. Again, you should know your horse's normal pulse rate. It can be taken either just behind the elbow or, more usually, by feeling along the inside of the bottom jaw.

A horse's normal respiration rate is between 8 and 16 breaths per minute, horses being nearer the lower end of the scale and ponies at the higher end. If the breathing is much faster than this the animal is probably in pain, and is likely to have a high temperature. A horse should not normally make a noise when breathing.

PREVENTIVE MEASURES

There are a number of preventive measures to help to ensure that a horse stays in good health.

Vaccinations

One of the most important vaccinations is an injection against tetanus, a serious disease to which horses are more susceptible than most other animals. The germ enters the horse's system through a wound, which can be no more than a tiny puncture in the skin. After an incubation period, the poison released acts directly on the central nervous system. As the disease progresses the horse is unable to open his mouth to eat (hence the disease's other name of "lock-jaw"), becomes stiff and stands with his forelegs pushed out in front and his hindlegs pushed out behind. Until quite recently the condition was usually terminal. Vaccination treatment of two injections four weeks apart, backed up by regular booster vaccinations produces long-lasting immunity. It is essential to protect a horse in this way.

Influenza is an extremely infectious disease which rapidly spreads through a stable yard. It is caused by a virus attacking the respiratory system, resulting in coughing and a weakening of the heart tissues (sufficient to be fatal to foals). Two initial vaccinations are needed, followed by a booster every year. Influenza vaccinations are now compulsory in many countries for all racehorses, show jumpers and eventers, as well as in other competitive fields, where a large number of horses may congregate together.

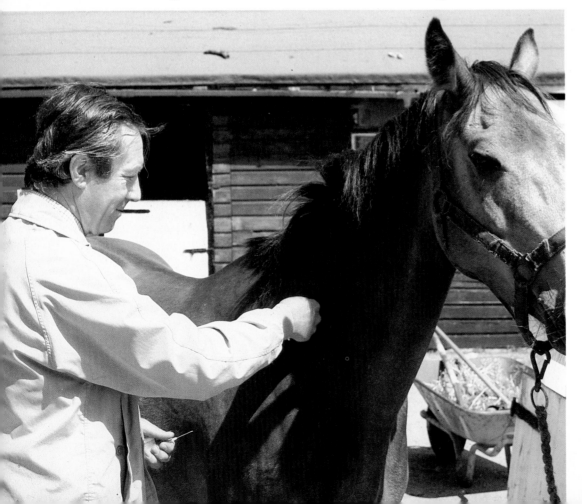

Left: The veterinary surgeon giving a routine anti-tetanus injection. It is essential to protect the horse in this way from this very serious disease which can be contracted through a tiny scratch on the skin.

Right: This gag device keeps the horse's mouth open while the vet examines his teeth and rasps any sharp edges. It looks dramatic but horses don't seem to mind.

Worms

This is a universal source of trouble. All horses have a degree of worm infestation, but it must be kept under strict control.

There are two main types of worm: ascarids or white worm, and strongyles or red worm. In moderation, ascarids do little harm in an adult horse, but if there are too many of them the horse will lose condition, the coat will stare and colic (equine stomach-ache) and respiratory problems can ensue. These worms can easily be seen in the droppings.

Strongyles cause considerably more problems. They pass through the intestine into the blood vessels, interrupting the blood supply to the intestine and in severe cases causing stoppages of the bloodstream, resulting in anemia, loss of condition and, in severely neglected cases, possible blockage of an artery.

Since worms are picked up by the horse when grazing, proper grass management can help in control. However, there is no way worms can ever be entirely eliminated from a pasture, so the final control must be within the horse. Various worming preparations are on the market, in paste, powder and pellet form, and all horses, whether stabled or at grass, should be treated regularly with one of these preparations. Vary the type occasionally to prevent worms building up an immunity, but consult with the veterinarian.

Teeth

Teeth problems can also result in the horse losing condition since if his teeth are painful he will be discouraged from chewing his food properly. Equally, when he is being ridden the bit may press against the small "wolf" teeth, present in some horses behind the incisors, causing discomfort and preventing the horse from responding as he should. Have the veterinarian check a horse's teeth annually to remove wolf teeth if necessary and to rasp any sharp points on the teeth which may have occurred through uneven wear.

FIRST AID KIT

All horse owners should keep a basic first aid kit close at hand so that common injuries and ailments can be dealt with promptly. It is best kept in a clean cupboard or box with all the items labeled, each one replaced when used or if it remains unused for too long.

A basic first aid kit should include the following:

Cotton wool – for cleaning wounds, sponging eyes and nostrils, etc.

Antiseptic lint – for dressing wounds.

Disinfectant – keep a bottle of diluted disinfectant handy

Elastic crêpe bandages – to keep dressings in place.

Vaseline (petroleum jelly) – useful for bit injuries, cracked heels, etc

Poultice – sealed foil packets of kaolin are now available which are easier to use than the traditional canned kaolin. Dry dressings, which have first to be soaked in water, are also widely used and can be applied hot or cold.

Antiseptic dusting powder – to put on a wound after cleaning.

Sterile tissue or non-stick pads – for use as padding to place over an open wound.

Surgical spirit – for hardening the skin after it has been rubbed bare.

Laxative salts – to add to a bran mash.

Liniment – for applying to swellings.

Tin of cough electuary

Thermometer, blunt-ended scissors and **bowl**

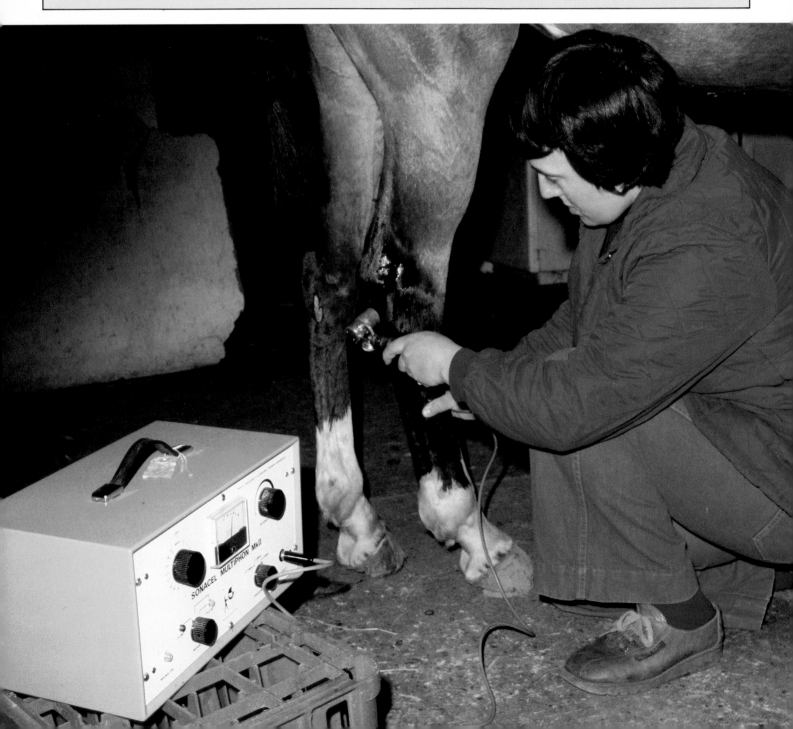

Wounds and injuries

Wounds can be divided into four types – cuts and tears, puncture wounds, deep wounds and bruises. Cuts and tears are probably the most common and can vary from a minor scratch through grazing, clean cuts caused by a sharp object such as glass, to tears where the skin is torn by something sharp, perhaps leaving a flap of skin that will need stitching. An "over-reach", when the hind shoe catches on the heel of the corresponding foreleg, ripping through the skin, is a common tear. Broken knees, occurring when the horse trips over on the road or other hard surface, breaking the skin over his knees and grazing them, is another example of a wound in this category. Often the hair does not grow back over this sort of injury, or if it does, it comes through white.

In all these cases the wound should be cleansed with cotton wool, clean water and disinfectant. If it is not deep it should then be dressed with antiseptic powder. In more serious cases, if it looks as if the wound needs stitching, call the veterinarian. He will also administer anti-tetanus serum if the horse is not already protected.

Puncture wounds tend to be more serious and can easily be missed; it is important, therefore, to check over a horse thoroughly each day. Leg wounds of this sort are frequently caused by thorns, or if in the foot the horse may have stepped on a nail or something similarly sharp. All wounds are more dangerous if they are near a joint, but never leave any wound untreated.

Deep wounds usually cause heavy bleeding, blood from a vein being a deep red color, while arterial blood is bright red and tends to spurt from the wound. In both cases bleeding should be stopped by applying pressure to the wound with a clean pad and holding this firmly in place either by hand or with a tight bandage (if practicable). The veterinarian should be called immediately.

Bruising is usually the result of a kick or other impact and is not always immediately noticeable. Kicks are more serious if directed at a leg bone or joint, rather than the better padded body area. Swelling and pain will be obvious; running cold water over the area helps reduce both. In some cases ultrasonic therapy is used to reduce hard swellings on the legs following a knock, but obviously this is a case for professional treatment.

Left: Ultrasonic radiation can help to reduce swellings following a knock, when applied for a few minutes each day. However, this is for professional use only.

Above: The horse's legs should be checked every day for lumps and swellings denoting possible injuries.

Below: A wire injury to the leg. Barbed wire, particularly when slack, should be avoided as a means of fencing.

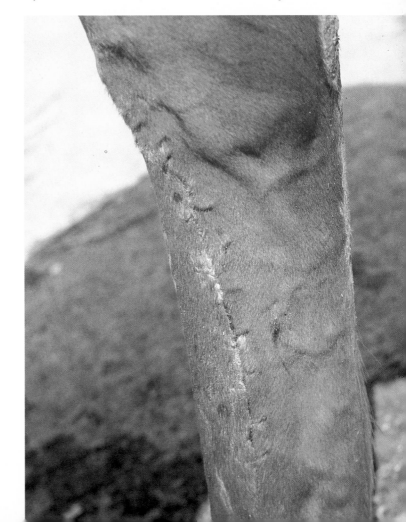

Galling

Rubbing and galling occurs in the mouth and saddle region and is caused by ill-fitting or dirty tack. Saddle and girth galls are sore patches on the skin where tack has rubbed the hair away, and in some cases may have broken the skin. A badly-fitting bit and/or rough hands on the reins will cause sores to the mouth.

Clean the area with fresh water and disinfectant; dust sores in the mouth and saddle region with antiseptic powder. Once the open wound has healed, the skin can be hardened by applying salt and water or surgical spirit.

In severe cases of saddle sores, the saddle may have pressed on the back to such an extent that blood circulation is restricted, and a portion of the skin dies as a result. This is a case for the veterinarian; in all cases of saddlery sores, the horse should not be ridden until the affected areas have healed.

Lameness

It is not always as easy as you might imagine to detect lameness. Except for the most obvious cases, it will be necessary to trot the horse out on hard level ground to determine which leg is paining him. In the case of suspected lameness in the forelegs, have the horse trotted towards you on a loose rein and note his head movement. If the head nods and falls noticeably, the lame leg will be the one on which the head is *raised*. If he seems to be lame in the hindlegs have him trotted away from you and watch the highest part of his quarters. If he is lame in either leg there will be a definite rise and fall of this part, the affected leg being the one on which the hip is *raised*. Unless you are very sure of the cause of the lameness and know how to treat it, contact your veterinarian.

The foot

When any lameness occurs start by examining the foot, as this is most often where the problem lies. Initially, feel for any heat, then for any area of sensitivity – which can be determined by picking up the hoof and tapping it firmly with a hammer. Examine both hind or both fore feet for comparison. If the horse flinches more on one foot than the other, call the farrier to remove the shoe, so that the foot can be examined thoroughly. Either the farrier or veterinarian can check for a bruised sole (the horse may have stepped on something hard, or perhaps have a stone wedged in his foot); or for corns which occur under the heels (usually of the fore feet) and are often caused by a badly-fitting shoe; or for a puncture wound – a result of treading on a nail; or following a visit from the farrier when it is possible that the sensitive laminae may accidentally have been pricked.

Intermittent lameness: This may be caused by changes in the bony structure of the foot and is determined by a "nerve block", in which the use of a local anesthetic over the nerve blocks out all pain. If the horse then gets better the problem is in the foot and an X-ray can be used to determine exactly what is wrong.

Navicular disease is probably the best known cause of intermittent lameness, and is usually apparent in forefeet that have been subjected to concussion. The animal "points" first one limb and then the other if both feet are affected, and moves on the toes of his forefeet. This condition can be treated with a certain measure of success by a veterinarian but it may constitute a permanent unsoundness. It affects the navicular bone, which is situated on the inner side of the foot.

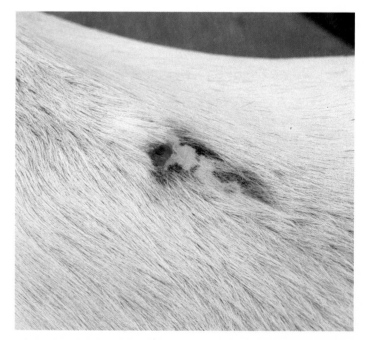

Left: This galling has been caused by rubbing from a roller or surcingle.

Above: An example of a bad saddle sore caused by ill-fitting (or dirty) tack.

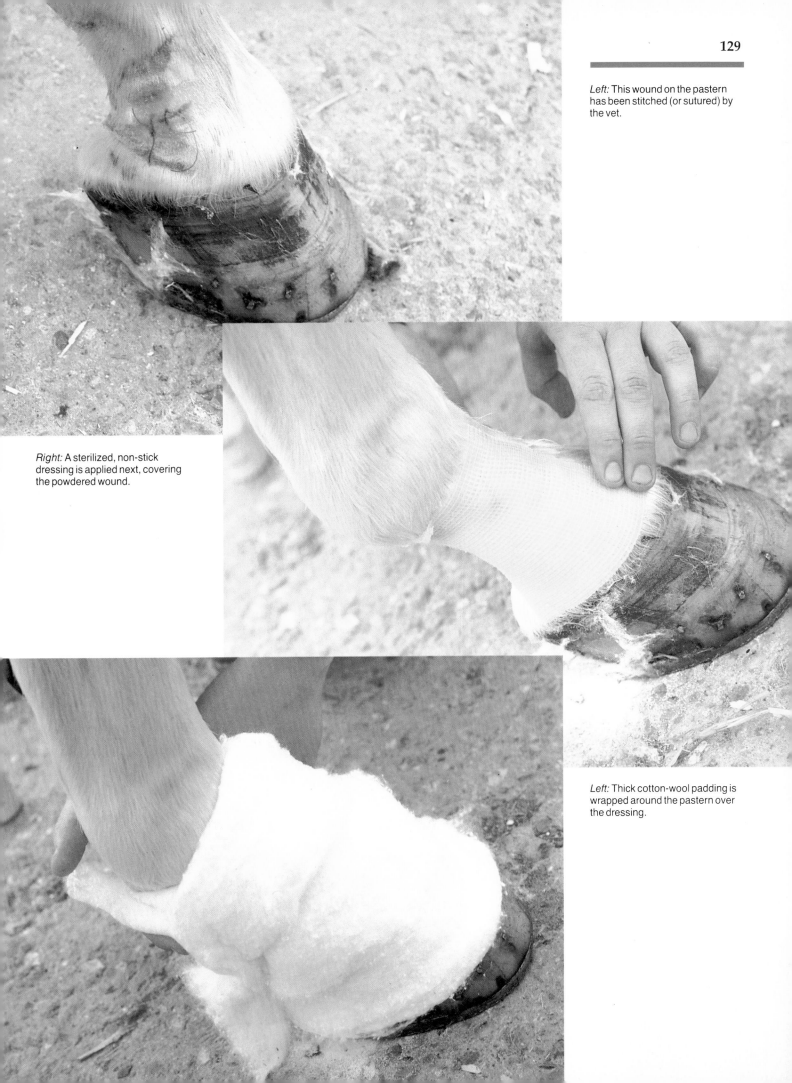

Left: This wound on the pastern has been stitched (or sutured) by the vet.

Right: A sterilized, non-stick dressing is applied next, covering the powdered wound.

Left: Thick cotton-wool padding is wrapped around the pastern over the dressing.

The Legs

If no troubles are found in the feet, examine the legs for heat, swellings and tenderness. A bony enlargement round the rop of the hoof or around the pastern bones indicates high and low ringbone respectively. This is a form of arthritis and lameness is progressive. The veterinarian may use painkilling drugs but the condition is chronic.

A bony enlargement may also occur higher up the leg on the cannon bone, just below the knee. This is a "splint" and occurs frequently on the forelegs of horses up to five years old. It does not always cause lameness although sometimes the animal will be lame for some weeks, perhaps becoming worse with exercise. Initially the area will feel hot and treatment involves rest and regular hosings with cold water. When the inflamed splint bone is set it no longer causes lameness, even though the "lump" remains and the horse can resume work.

Spavin: A bony enlargement on the inside of the hindleg, on the hock, is called a spavin. The horse tends to drag the toe rather than lift it clear of the ground and, although lameness is intermittent initially, the horse will become progressively more lame until the bony growths have become fused. Initial rest, followed by gentle exercise, will encourage the arthritic bones to set. When this happens the horse will become sound again.

Strains: If there are no bony enlargements on the legs, lameness may be caused by a strained tendon. The area around the tendons will be warm and painful to the touch. It may be the tendon sheath alone which is affected (tenovitis) or the tendon itself may be damaged (strained tendon), but both (the latter a more serious form of the former) are caused by overstretching the tendon. Complete rest is the only cure. Rest is, indeed, the first requirement with any form of lameness.

Laminitis: If there is unusual heat in the foot, particularly in the forefeet, and the horse is acutely lame, it is quite likely that he has laminitis or fever in the foot. This is particularly prevalent in fat ponies living out on rich grazing when the new grass comes through in the spring, but it can also be caused by galloping on hard ground, when the animal is unfit. The horse will stand with both front feet stretched out forward of the normal stance in an effort to take the weight off them, and ridges around the hoof may also be noticeable. His feed should be cut drastically and cold water applied to the feet. Consult the veterinarian, who may advise anti-inflammatory agents as a short-term measure.

Thrush: This is an infection of the soft horn of the frog of the foot which occurs when the horse is left to stand for hours on end on wet, dirty bedding. The frog becomes soft and has a fetid odor accompanied by heat and inflammation in the foot. To cure the infection, remove the wet conditions permanently, have the farrier pare away the infected horn, and apply a strong antiseptic to the infected region.

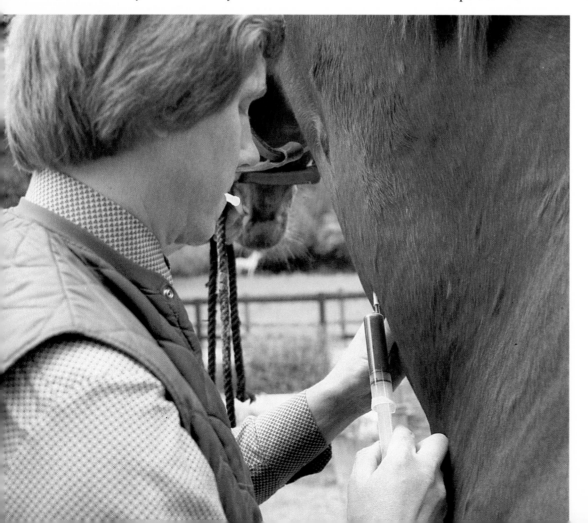

Left: Vets' time is expensive, but often professional advice is essential for the well-being of the horse. Here a vet is taking a blood sample from the large jugular vein in the horse's neck.

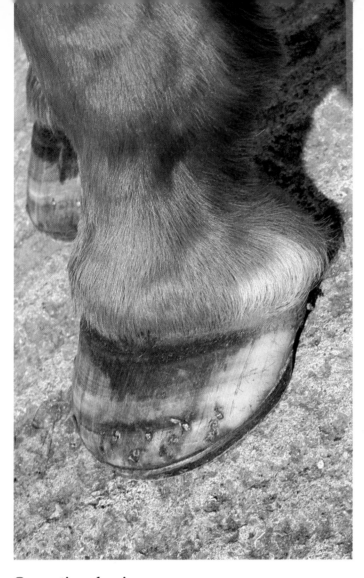

Left: A foot showing signs of laminitis. Note the horizontal rings running round the hoof; severe lameness and unusual heat in the foot are other indications.

Above: There are a variety of remedial shoes which can be fitted to alleviate lameness.

Below: A foot shod with leather between hoof and shoe to help prevent jarring on the foot.

Corrective shoeing

In many cases of lameness or just faulty action, corrective shoeing can alleviate the situation. As a warning to buyers, it can also hide conformation defects.

Horses suffering from navicular disease (see page 128), for instance, cannot accept pressure on the frog as the diseased navicular bone lies just above it. Shoes which are thicker at the heels and with the toes rolled help to reduce the pressure, and thus the pain. Laminitis sufferers who have sensitive soles benefit from being shod with a seated shoe, where a gap is left between shoe and foot on the inside of the shoe in order to shift the bearing surface to the outside wall. Soft pads between shoe and foot can also be used to help against jarring, as can a piece of leather across the foot, held in place by the shoe.

"Three-quarter bar" shoes which transfer the pressure on to the frog are often used in cases of corns, whereas high wedge heels and a rolled toe may help to relieve strain in the case of spavins.

For a horse recovering from strained tendons, shoes that are thickened at the heel lessen the strain imposed on the tendons. Pattern shoes which incorporate a raised bar set across the heel can be used on occasions to relieve tendon strain, but these have to be removed and the height altered very frequently if the tendons are not to retract.

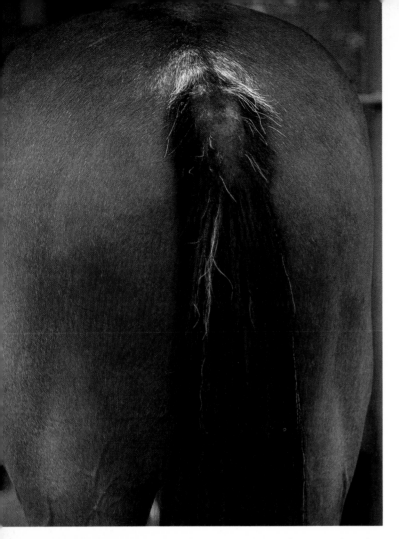

Above: Sweet itch has caused this badly rubbed tail. Note how the new tail hairs have come through white.

Skin diseases

Sweet Itch: This is an allergic dermatitis caused by midges biting the horse, usually at dawn and dusk during the summer months. The midges attack the mane and base of the tail of the animal. Once a horse has become allergic to the bites, he will always remain so and the irritation is so intense that he will rub the mane and tail until raw and hairless. As midges attack early and late in the day, horses that suffer from their bites should be stabled at these times. Fly repellents may help to discourage midges if applied regularly and the veterinarian can supply anti-inflammatory drugs to ease the irritation.

Ringworm: This is a fungal infection of the skin, so highly contagious that it is important to keep a set of tack, clothing, grooming kit and so on for the exclusive use of an affected animal. Ringworm can affect any part of the skin and causes small patches of bare skin, usually crusty and circular in shape, to appear. The veterinarian will supply antibiotics to kill off the fungus. Humans too can be infected with this condition.

Warbles: Warble fly larvae migrate through the horse's legs to the back and emerge through the skin, forming a permanent swelling. Initially they are painful and, if they appear in the saddle region, the horse should not be ridden. In some instances the swellings disappear of their own accord, leaving a blemish, but if they are persistent, call the veterinarian to remove the larvae surgically.

Mud Fever and Cracked Heels: Both of these complaints are skin irritations caused by muddy and wet conditions. Mud fever affects the legs, making them hot and swollen with a thin discharge coming from cracks in the skin, while cracked heels, as the name suggests, manifests in sore, chapped heels. In both cases the areas must be kept dry, any scabs removed and an antiseptic solution applied to the affected areas. A waterproof barrier cream can then be applied to the affected areas on occasions when it is unavoidable for the horse to be turned out in the wet.

Digestive complaints

Colic: This is a severe stomach-ache that can be caused by a number of things, among them worms, sudden changes in diet, eating poor-quality food, eating too much or taking a long drink after a large feed. The horse will look around at his flanks, paw the ground and probably begin sweating. He may then get down and try to roll. The pulse rate will probably increase and the breathing be labored. The veterinarian should be called immediately. Keep the horse warm and walk him to prevent him from injuring himself.

Respiratory diseases

Coughs: Horses are prone to coughs that can be caused by all sorts of reasons, among them lack of ventilation when stabled, from dusty hay, or by being kept in the stable after being turned out for some time. A cough that is accompanied by a thin, clear nasal discharge is best treated by giving cough electuary on the tongue, and keeping the horse warm, while providing plenty of ventilation. If the cough is accompanied by a thick discharge, an increased breathing rate and rise in temperature it is probably caused by a lung infection and the veterinarian should be called. If the cough is a dry one caused by dusty hay, discard your current stocks and buy hay of better quality. If the cough persists even then, wet the hay thoroughly, letting it drain before feeding. Never work a coughing horse.

Broken wind: This may follow a chronic cough or other lung disease. It is marked by a harsh, dry cough, accompanied by nasal discharge, labored breathing and the flanks appearing to heave *twice* on exhalation. There is little hope of a cure but the veterinarian may be able to alleviate the situation.

When describing an animal's condition to the veterinarian, be as accurate as possible. You will be speaking for your horse and indeed for yourself, for both of you will suffer if you give misleading information leading to wrong diagnosis.

Try to understand the problems that the veterinarian has to face. Remember, too, that although a veterinarian often has a longer, tougher training than a doctor, he still needs your help in identifying the symptoms that led to you calling him out.

A Haflinger mare, with the distinctive chestnut coat and flaxen mane and tail, grazing peacefully with her young foal in their native homeland of the Austrian Tyrol.

HORSES IN ACTION

Above: These gray Shires are a major attraction at the annual Horse of the Year Show in England where they combine their musical drive with harrowing the jumping arena.

Right: The Windsor grays drawing the open carriage after the wedding of HRH The Prince of Wales and Lady Diana Spencer. The escort is made up of the Life Guards and the Blues and Royals.

THE WORKING HORSE

What is meant by the term working horse? The dividing line between a so-called working horse and one used, say, for leisure or sport is fine, but basically a working horse is one that is put to use to help man in his own work. He may be a working horse one week and used for sporting the next. It follows that a sporting horse is one that is used for our own pleasure, although we may not ask him to be involved in competitive sport.

The Heavies

Draught horses – in danger of extinction until recently – have made a huge comeback, and not just in the show ring. Shires, Percherons, Suffolks, Ardennes and Clydesdales, not to mention numerous smaller animals of mixed or unknown breeding, are still pulling carts and wagons, timber and even plows on farms throughout North America and Europe.

Although tractors have taken over much of the major work in the USA, small farmers are still finding that horse-drawn agricultural equipment can do as good a job or better than modern methods, particularly on very heavy ground or steep hills. Single horses, pairs, and teams of up to eight, coupled together via the complicated multiple hitching system developed in the mid-western corn belts, all have their place beside the farmer.

Even on big farms, horses are used to take fodder to stock grazing in fields too far from the feed storage to be reached by foot. Pulling lumber offers these big, docile animals a chance to earn their keep not just across farmland, but in logging camps everywhere; and in maple syrup country – New England and Canada – horsepower again proves the most effective means of transporting the golden liquid from the trees to the processing point.

Farm horses haven't changed much since their heyday only 50 to 100 years ago: they still need to be strong (although not necessarily big) and placid. Good horses are in great demand, with many imported from Europe. In 1984, for instance, 63 English Shires were brought into Canada and the United States.

In Europe, a tradesman delivering milk, bread, coal and so on with his horse-and-float or cart was once a common sight. Today, of course, these everyday commodities are delivered by motor transportation, but many breweries operating in towns and urban areas are continuing the traditions of using heavy horses to make their deliveries. Apart from the economic factor which they claim to be viable, it has proved to be useful publicity for the breweries to have their smartly turned out drays doing the daily round. By and large, the tradesman's trap and coster's cart are now reserved for parades and displays – the Harness Horse Parade which takes place in London's Regents Park every Easter is one of the best known of these events in Britain.

In Australia, New Zealand and South America, stock horses are a valuable means of transport for overseeing cattle and sheep on the vast outback lands, often impenetrable to the automobile. In the USSR herdsmen tend their herds of horses from horseback as do the *Czikos* of Hungary. In underdeveloped countries, where there is often plenty of unused land onto which horses, donkeys and mules can be set to graze, the peasants still largely rely on these animals for personal and pack transport.

Left: Here a pair of Shires draw a binder. Small farmers still find that horse-drawn agricultural equipment can do as good a job or better than modern methods.

Right: In less developed countries, rural communities still rely largely on ponies to transport themselves and their belongings.

Left: A pair of Percherons at the English National Plowing Championships, showing how plowing was traditionally carried out, the plowman guiding the plow behind.

Left: The tradesman's trap is now largely reserved for parades and displays; motorized transportation has taken over the deliveries – except for some breweries. This is a nineteenth-century horsebus.

Out on the Ranch

The branding iron may be powered by electricity instead of campfire flames and calves may go to market by truck instead of on their own four hooves, but all the progress in the Western world cannot take the place of the working cow pony. There is really no other way to work cattle, to bring them into the corral and separate them one by one from the herd, than by using the horse.

A typical ranch may farm 250 head of cattle over 2000 acres. Trucks cannot travel much of the country which the cattle call home and, although they are used to check some of the herds and fences, if the rancher wants to round up escaped cattle or search for a missing cow, the horse is the best means of traveling through bush and up rocky hills.

The highlight of the working cow horse's year is the round-up. A ranch's entire stock is brought in over a short period, usually only three days, for pregnancy tests on the cows, vaccination, ear-tagging and branding of any new calves.

Working cow ponies tend to be small, averaging 15 h.h., even-tempered and sensible. Quarter Horses are still widely used as they are placid, tractable, tough and have an innate "cow-sense". Cow ponies must be able to fend for themselves and live on grass alone, supplemented by hay in winter. Tough feet are essential, as they work unshod, and they must look out for holes and other dangers of the terrain themselves to enable the cowboys to concentrate on the job at hand. They must also be brave enough to enter a herd of sometimes frightened cattle, and understand the cattle's nature enough to be able to anticipate every move.

Below: A working horse on a Texas ranch, where horses are still used to work cattle.

Right: A police horse competes at the Horse of the Year Show, faced with a simulated riot.

The Police Horse

In most parts of the world crowd control, that delicate and difficult task, was first carried out (usually with a minimum of consideration for the crowd itself) by the "military" – dragoons or local yeomanry. In Britain, the pioneer, the control of large and possibly unruly gatherings of people by civil police began in 1805 when the London "Bow Street Patrol" was formed. Its aim was to guard and patrol the main roads within 20 miles (30 kilometers) of Bow Street, which in effect was the entire London region of the day. Later the Metropolitan Police Force took over and, because of its great success, was copied by the larger cities all over Great Britain, and eventually by many major capitals throughout the world.

The city police horse is not likely to be supplanted in the foreseeable future, as it can be more effective in handling crowds, from hot-tempered gangs of soccer fans to near-rioting mobs, than the armored cars, water cannon or tear gas that may be used elsewhere.

In London, the 400 horses used by the Metropolitan area and the City of London Mounted Police have a gala day every year in November at the Lord Mayor's Show, where they are at the head and rear of the ornate parade. The Metropolitan Mounted Division also supply almost all the horses ridden by the members of the Royal Family at the Trooping of the Colour Ceremony which marks Her Majesty Queen Elizabeth's official birthday.

Every year each horse returns to the training headquarters of the mounted police force for a refresher course and it is at these that the horses learn to jump through various hazards, to ignore loud music and every other sort of noisy horror, and to accept heavy traffic. Bravery, strength and a cool head in every situation are as important for the police horse as for his rider. Nothing frightens the average horse more than a pushing, screaming throng of people coupled with police car sirens and loudspeakers, yet police horses on crowd control duty not only must stand still amid such chaos, but also be ready and prepared to go forward into the very thing they would normally run away from.

Not all police horse duties are so onerous, though; they may be used, instead, to cross country inaccessible by car in search of a criminal or missing child, but they most frequently serve simply as the policeman's partner, carrying him around the streets of his beat.

The most famous mounted police force in the world is undoubtedly the Royal Canadian Mounted Police, formed in the remote north-western districts of the country, where horses were the only means of transport. The "Mounties" began breeding their own horses in 1940, opting for animals that have a lot of Thoroughbred blood, are fairly big – 16 h.h. plus – and are black or dark brown. The force is no longer operational as such, but is still seen extensively performing its famous musical ride at shows and displays. Mounted police in the USA use "any horse that's a good one", and smaller animals are often seen there. Morgans are particularly favored because of their steady nature and tough physical attributes.

The Warhorse

The horse has a long history as an instrument of war, used by all cultures throughout the world. The Nubians of ancient Egyptian times used horses in battle, the Greeks used them long before the stirrup was invented, and Attila the Hun found them more useful than the elephants he laboriously marched over the Alps to terrorize ancient Rome.

Medieval knights were perhaps the first to use cavalry in an organized way, making disciplined charges against the enemy. Their mounts were the massive horses that have since developed into the modern heavy draught horse. These horses needed every muscle they possessed to carry the dead weight of the metal armor of their overloaded riders. In general, foot soldiers could manage to defeat this ponderous clanking cavalry, for once the horseman was unseated he was at a huge disadvantage in his crushingly heavy armor.

The development of firearms in the fourteenth century changed the tactics. Direct charges were out, and the fire-from-a-moving-target technique became fashionable. A mounted troop would trot to within pistol range of the opposing force, turn parallel to it, fire off a round at the enemy, and then wheel away to reload. This technique is similar to the legendary tactics used later by mounted American Indians and, as it was an effective system of attack, it gave rise to the circle of wagons as defense some 300 years before the classic scenes of the American West took place.

As artillery developed and faster horses were bred, guns and limbers were towed into battle by large teams of horses. In the seventeenth century, the first Royal mounted bodyguards were formed by England's King Charles II, who created the "first mounted troops of Britain's standing army", the Life Guards. These were original Household Cavalry, which one may still see daily on guard duty in London.

Today the role of the cavalry is principally a ceremonial one (although the riders are fully operational serving soldiers), the Life Guards and the Blues and Royals being the Queen's escort for all ceremonial occasions as well as performing guard duties. In addition to the 200-odd black horses stabled at the barracks in London there are twelve or so gray trumpet horses and six big 17 h.h. piebald or skewbald horses – the drum horses who march at the head of the mounted bands.

Stars of the Screen

Horses are a vital part of the modern movie industry, although their names may not appear on the credits. Few equine screen stars have matched Trigger, Champion or the Lone Ranger's Silver. One good, trained horse, it is said, is worth 50 extras, not just in thousands of Western movies, but in any movie set in pre-automobile days, as well as in popular television series like **Dallas**.

Most film horses are only required to have an even temperament so that they can be ridden or driven by people lacking expert horse experience. Others, however, must stand still in a huge crowd, ignore gunshots, fire and other distractions, leap over gaping chasms and, the most valuable skill of all, be able to fall without hurting themselves or their riders.

In order to provide the volume of skilled horses needed by the fast-developing Hollywood industry, a number of training ranches sprang up in California in the early part of this century, often staffed by genuine cowboys. Although some early methods of training and using horses in films caused suffering and even death to the animals concerned, the American Humane Association and SPCA brought about changes which made the horse's life a happier one. Good horse trainers have always relied, though, on the trust and affection of their animals rather than on cruelty to achieve results.

Above: A London scene: the Life Guards, who perform guard duties in addition to their ceremonial duties as the Queen's escort.

Left: British tradition. The King's Troop of the Royal Horse Artillery pulling a gun-carriage in Regents Park in central London.

Right: Roy Rogers and his famous four-legged partner Trigger. Rogers trained Trigger to perform many tricks, including galloping to save the hero in the nick of time.

The Circus

The circus ring provides a perfect setting for the horse. Under the bright lights of the big top, immaculately turned out with sparkling trappings and feathered plumes, the beautifully schooled horses are a big hit with young and old audiences alike. Breeds used in circus work include Lipizzaners, Andalusians, Arabians, the spotted Knabstrupers, Shetlands, Welsh and others.

The first circus was started in London by Philip Astley, but today the circus is more popular on the European continent. Circus Knie has one of the largest troupes of horses in Switzerland and the Circque Rancy is one of the biggest in France. In Germany, one of the most famous is Circus Knone, but the biggest in the world is still the Ringling Brothers Barnum & Bailey in America that at one time took over some of the horses – mainly Lipizzaners and Arabians – belonging to the British circus of Billy Smart.

Below: Immaculately turned out circus horses with their sparkling trappings and feathered plumes are always a hit with circus audiences all over the world.

Tourists and Publicity

A sightseer in the elegant Champs-Elyseé in Paris will still be able to find, amongst the hordes of Citroën taxis and buzzing Renaults, an occasional horse-drawn *fiacre*, a French hire-cab, slowly trotting down the road. The wise old horse will be oblivious of the mechanical traffic hurling itself down the wide boulevard and its driver, hunched in his high seat, will look like a character from a Lautrec poster of the nineteenth century.

In Bruges and Amsterdam, Rome and Vienna, these tourist carriages still ply their sleepy trade, and visitors from other, faster-moving environments love to use this form of conveyance to see the sights. In many of Europe's winter resorts, the evening sleigh ride is still the chic way to spend an apres-ski hour, with a couple of Haflingers in the shafts, trotting over snow-covered tracks past wooden chalets and through dark green forests. In Egypt the easiest way to get from the antiquities at Karnak to those at Luxor is still to take a horse-drawn "gharry" trip alongside the Nile, and in New York's Central Park nothing is more romantic than a carriage ride on a summer's evening.

Left: Seeing the sights by horse-drawn carriage is a must for tourists. This is the city of Quebec, Canada.

Above: Riding along a sandy beach provides a pleasant relaxation for the vacationer in Jamaica.

The number of horses still pulling all kinds of vehicles as an integral part of their owner's livelihood remains substantial enough throughout the world to remind us of the age when horses were the only means of transport. In some areas horses are still used to carry the family on Sundays or in snowy weather; the Amish community, or Pennsylvania Dutch, which turns its back on automotive products, uses the horse-drawn trap to carry produce to market as well as to take the family to church and the children to school.

Gaily-painted vehicles pulled by a handsome steed, pair or team advertises.many a company in parades or carnivals, and even just on daily exercise, perhaps making a few deliveries. Budweiser's magnificent Clydesdales are perhaps the most famous advertising equines in the USA, but businesses of all sizes and in all locations have discovered that heads turn when a horse walks by, and those turning heads just might remember the name painted on the side of the wagon.

Hunting is a highly popular country activity attracting a wide following both in Europe and in America. It has had an influence on steeple chasing and also point-to-point.

THE SPORTING HORSE

The most popular equestrian sports – those whose greatest exponents are household names – are racing and show-jumping, but there are many other equestrian activities which provide satisfying sport at many different levels for the avid rider looking for competitive opportunity. An introduction to the world of competition at juvenile level is provided in many countries through mounted or gymkhana games, and it is not unusual for adults to participate in some versions of these games as is shown by the police and the army, who still conduct "tent-pegging" and "skill-at-arms" competitions in many countries.

Racing

Of all equestrian sports, it is racing – flat racing in particular – that has attracted the elite and the wealthy from all over the world. While testing the speed of one horse against that of another is a competitive sport almost as old as riding itself, "organized" racing can be traced to the England of James I.

Since that time, the British Royal Family have continued, on and off, to take an active interest in the "sport of kings". James I "discovered" the now well-known racing town of Newmarket as a center for hunting, hawking and racing in 1605, and 60 years later, Charles II founded the Newmarket Town Plate – a famous race in which he also rode and won twice himself.

Newmarket has been the home of flat racing in England ever since this time, with the headquarters of the Jockey Club, the governing body and world-recognized "turf authority", situated there. Two of the five English Classic races, the 2000 Guineas and the 1000 Guineas, are both held in Newmarket over a "straight mile" (1.6 km). The 2000 Guineas is for colts and fillies and was first run in 1809, while the 1000 Guineas is for fillies only and was introduced five years later.

Queen Anne founded the most fashionable of the English racecourses – Ascot – in 1711, and the four-day Royal meeting is strongly supported by members of the Royal Family today.

The "Blue Riband of the Turf", the 200-year-old English Derby run at Epsom is regarded as one of the greatest tests for three-year-olds and is open to colts and fillies. Initially run over 1 mile (1.6 km), but now over 1½ miles (2.4 km), it is undoubtedly one of the British Classics.

Races for three-year-olds are possibly the most famous internationally. The other English Classics are the Oaks, open only to fillies and also run at Epsom over 1½ miles (2.4 km), and the St. Leger, open to both colts and fillies and run each year at Doncaster. This, in fact, is the oldest of these Classic races, being first run in 1776.

Horse-racing has been popular in America since the early settlers matched their horses against one another down the dusty dirt tracks of their properties.

However, the first organized racecourse seems to have been a 2 mile (3.2 km) track on Hempstead Plain, Long Island, near Belmont Park, New York. It is this latter venue which is the home of the famous Belmont Stakes, inaugurated in 1867, one of the three races comprising the American Triple Crown. The other two are the Preakness Stakes, inaugurated in 1873 and run on the Pimlico course in Maryland and the Kentucky Derby run at Churchill Downs, Louisville, Kentucky.

Before the Civil War, Virginia and New York were the leading racing centers, but ever since 1865 the Blue Grass country of Kentucky has been the prominent racing area. A member of the Rothschild banking family, August Belmont, helped establish the modern racehorse industry in Kentucky and he was to become president of the American Jockey Club in 1917. His son, August Belmont II, bred the legendary racehorse Man-O-War, known popularly as Big Red or "The Mostest Horse" – a horse that won 20 out of the 21 races he ran. This amazing horse was appointed Honorary Colonel in the US Army's First Cavalry Division, and on his death became the first horse in modern history to be embalmed. His only real rival in popularity since came over 50 years later, from the beautiful chestnut, Secretariat, who was the first horse to win the American Triple Crown in a quarter of a century. His total winnings for the 1973 three-year-old season amounted to a staggering $1,860,404.

Flat racing in America is principally concerned with two-year-olds and "sprinting" races, although distance racing is popular with many of the racing fraternity. Racetracks vary from ½ to 1½ miles (0.8 to 2.4 km) in circumference, and many of them offer superb facilities to spectators. Usually nine or ten races are held per meeting.

Below: Horse-racing has been popular in America since the days of the early settlers. Most races are held on dirt tracks like this one in Miami, Florida.

The rest of the racing world owes a great debt to American racing for producing the jockey who was to revolutionize the "racing seat". In the early days of racing, a jockey rode like any other horseman, balanced across the horse's back, his seat in the saddle and his legs supported by the stirrup irons hanging long either side of the animal's ribs. Towards the end of the nineteenth century, an American jockey called Todhunter Sloan invented the "monkey seat". It grew out of his observations of some stable lads having a bit of fun trying to kneel on their horse's backs, but Sloan noticed that the horses could move faster and more freely as a result. He shortened his stirrup leathers and crouched low on his horse's neck, and the racing seat was born. Those who frowned upon it initially soon adopted it when they saw Tod Sloan's success.

Racing is popular nearly worldwide. In Europe, France is probably the major country to be considered. The famous Prix de L'Arc de Triomphe takes place each year at Longchamps and attracts an international gathering of professionals and amateurs interested in the sport. It is a race for three-year-olds – taking place over 2 miles (3.2 km) – and is indeed one of the richest of all races. In Switzerland, racing at St. Moritz has an extra element of romance as it is run on snow. The oldest race in Canada, the Toronto Queens, was inaugurated by William IV in 1836, while in Australia the most famous race is the Melbourne Hunt Cup, run over 2 miles (3.2 km) at Flemington Racecourse. Races at Randwick racecourse in Sydney never fail to attract a large crowd and the Thoroughbred industry in Australia is one of the country's major businesses. Hong Kong, New Zealand, South America and India are just some of the other countries where racing has a large and active following.

Although Thoroughbred breeding and racing began in, and was dominated for some time by, England, there is no doubt that other countries – the United States of America and France, in particular – are forces to be reckoned with and have provided numbers of classic winners. The racehorse itself has become a truly international animal.

Left: The most famous steeplechase is the British Grand National at Aintree. Here two jockeys have come to grief at the Chair fence, which claims many victims.

Above: Harness-racing, for trotters and pacers, rivals flat-racing in popularity in America. This shows a trotter in Palm Beach, Forida, with its lightweight sulky.

Harness Racing

In the USA harness racing rivals flat racing in popularity, and the breed that excels in this sport is the American Standardbred. Both trotters and pacers are used in racing, and the latter – once considered to be the poor relation of the trotter – is generally slightly faster. The Standardbred actually takes its name from the standard time which, in the old days, a harness horse was expected to cover the distance of a mile (1.6 km). Today, this is 2 minutes 20 seconds.

Harness racing in America is undoubtedly the oldest form of horseracing, but arising informally as it did in races between working horses, it suffered somewhat when automobiles arrived on the scene and the number of working horses dropped drastically. It began a recovery in popularity in the 1930s and was aided by the formation of the United States Trotting Association in 1939. The rise in popularity continued as night racing under strong floodlights and the

mobile starting gate were introduced in the 1940s, both at New York's Roosevelt Raceway. Today races are usually held on a wide oval cinder track, usually over 1 mile (1.6 km) and custom-built, lightweight sulky vehicles are used – a far cry from the early days of the sport, when those impromptu races were held on the dirt roads.

Harness racing is popular in a number of other countries, notably New Zealand, the USSR and France, but also in Italy, Germany, Holland, Denmark and Scandinavia. In New Zealand, enthusiasts import Standardbreds from America to cross with native mares, and it was such a cross that produced the famous horse Cardigan Bay, which paced the mile in under two minutes.

In Russia, trotting racing is the popular sport of the Orlov Trotter first bred towards the end of the eighteenth century. Moscow's first trotting races were held in 1799 and its popularity has hardly wavered since. In the harsh winters, sledges on runners are often used behind the horses instead of the light carts. Harness racing came later to France than it did to the United States and USSR, the first trotting race being held in Paris in 1806, but such was its popularity that France also produced its own breed of trotting racehorse – the French trotter.

Steeplechasing

Steeplechasing is the racing of ridden horses over a course with fences. The sport began in that great country of horses – Ireland – where the first recognized race was held in 1752 over a 4½ mile (7.2 km) course from Buttevant Church to the spire or steeple of the church of St. Leger; hence the name "steeplechase". Informal dashes across country from the sight of one steeple to another (or merely from one specified point to another) had been common in Ireland before this time, and were common in England too – there was a famous one between two hunting men in Leicestershire in 1779 – but the first properly organized modern-style steeplechase in England was held in Bedford in 1810. The course was 3 miles (4.8 km) long and contained eight obstacles.

In America, during the late eighteenth and early nineteenth centuries, "pounding" races were held in Maryland, and it is here that the USA's principal steeplechase, the Maryland Hunt Cup, is still run. This was first held in 1894 when it was a tough race between members of the Elkridge Hunt and the Green Spring Valley Hunt. It is no less tough today, run over 4 miles (6.4 km) with a total of 22 very respectable fences to be jumped. One of the star performers in this race was the three-times winner (1963, 1964 and 1966) Jay Trump. In the year that he did not win – 1965 – he competed instead in the English Grand National, and to everyone's surprise and delight, won that too.

The Grand National, held at Aintree in the north of England in the spring, is probably the most famous steeplechase in the world. It was founded in 1837 by an

innkeeper who conceived the idea of holding a steeplechase. This race did not become known as the Grand National until sometime later. In its early days it was run over a number of hurdles and gorse-covered banks, a 5 ft (1.5 m) high wall and two brooks, one of which is the notorious Becher's Brook of today's course, named after a Captain Becher who fell there. The race today is extremely grueling, run over 4 miles (6.4 km), with 30 fences at least 4½ ft (1.4 m) high. It always claims its share of victims, but is still immensely popular with both riders and spectators.

The point-to-point race is the amateur form of steeplechasing, and was also first run as a private match between friends from one point to another. It grew out of the eighteenth century hunting field in England and even when it became an "organized" as opposed to an impromptu race, the meeting was restricted to only one race for members of the Hunt, riding the horses on which they regularly hunted. Today, it has undoubtedly become much more "professional", but it is still wholly aligned to the hunting scene and all competing horses must have been "regularly and fairly hunted" during the preceding season. All point-to-points are staged by hunts and there is always a race just for members. Other races include those for adjacent hunts as well as an open race for point-to-point horses from all over the country. While maintaining an amateur status, the sport nevertheless comes under the auspices of Jockey Club legislation.

Below and insert: Another famous steeplechase meeting is the three-day Spring fixture at Cheltenham, England.

Hunting

Hunting is certainly a sport, but a wholly non-competitive one. However, as it has had such an influence on other competitive sports – point-to-point and steeplechasing as we have seen, and also cross-country jumping events – it should be included here. It is still a highly popular country activity, although it is increasingly a subject of controversy and not a little militant demonstration by those who oppose it. It is still, perhaps, also a sport patronized by those who are able to afford the high costs it demands; those of keeping a horse in condition through the hunting season, as well as the annual subscription. Such people were once the "landed gentry", the landowners of the eighteenth and nineteenth centuries, when hunting in England and Ireland was really in its heyday. Today it attracts a far wider mix of hunt members than ever before.

Hunting with horses is another sport that is as old as riding itself – although it was originally done for necessity rather than sport, and well established by the eleventh century when it was the hare and the deer who were the principal quarries. Foxhunting did not really begin until the eighteenth century when, with the coming of the Enclosure Acts and the consequent dividing up of the country, hunting itself became a more organized sport.

Foxhunting spread to America and Canada, where today a hundred or more packs of foxhounds have a strong following. George Washington was an avid follower of the hunt and established a pack at Mount Vernon, to hunt along the Potomac river, with some hounds he was given by France (also a place where hunting, but mainly stag-hunting, is popular). The first organized Hunt Club in the USA was the Gloucester Foxhunting Club, founded in 1766 and said to contain "the best English blood" (of hounds). Red and gray foxes are hunted in the eastern states, and in the west the coyote is also hunted. All sorts of terrain and obstacles are encountered, from the solid timber fences of the Maryland grasslands, to the more rugged country of the canyons of California and Colorado. Middleburg, near Washington, is considered to be the center of hunting in the USA.

Below: Jumping courses include a variety of bright-colored poles, walls and waterjumps; many an ingenious course can be built by using just the five basic types of fence.

Jumping, Eventing and Dressage

A sport which owes at least some of its current great popularity to television coverage is show-jumping. Once confined to good-weather seasons, show-jumping is now an all-year-round sport, the winter season taking place under cover in a series of indoor jumping shows.

In spite of its popularity and its "big-business" aspect, show-jumping is a relative newcomer in the world of equestrian sports, with the first organized competitions being held in the 1860s. In Ireland the first Royal Dublin Horse Show in 1868 staged competitions for the "high leap" and the "wide leap". These were popular, and jumping competitions spread rapidly to France and Switzerland, Germany and Italy, with the first classes for international competitors being held in Turin in 1901.

These early classes have little in common with the exciting situations of today that have spectators – both at the show and watching television in their homes – sitting on the edges of their seats in anticipation. The courses themselves were extremely uninspiring, generally comprising an equal number of fences down each side of the ring with perhaps the water jump or a triple bar in the center. The white-painted fences had wooden slats resting on top of them which fell all too easily, giving none of the excitement that occurs when a rider today hits a fence and it trembles on the edge before either falling or staying in place. Penalties were awarded for touching a jump, with more if the horse knocked it with a foreleg rather than a hind. So complicated did this method of scoring prove to be that the outcome of a competition was quite often largely a matter of opinion! Time – one of the critical factors that makes today's competitions such nail-biting affairs – played no part, and competitors were allowed to circle in front of a fence if they felt their approach was wrong – a move that would count as a refusal in today's rules.

Since 1921, international jumping competitions have been regulated by the *Fédération Equestre Internationale*, which lays down rules regarding sizes of fences and time allowed, as well as giving guidelines to the course-builders for different types of competitions. All of this helped greatly in improving the standard of courses and competitions.

Today, while a course usually incorporates only the five types of fence – upright, parallel, staircase, pyramid and the water jump – the interpretations and combinations of the course-builder are ingenious. In addition, the bright colors of today's poles mixed with various flowering shrubs and bushes make any show-jumping course a far cry from those drab early courses. There are numerous jumping competitions held for all grades and standards of horse and pony at shows the world over. Countries that compete internationally include the USA, Great Britain, West Germany, France, Canada, Belgium, Switzerland, Italy, Holland, Australia, New Zealand, Ireland and some in South America.

Above: Show-jumping is a relative newcomer to the world of equestrian sports, but its popularity is such that there are competitions for all grades of horses and ponies.

Eventing could be described as the supreme test of skill and endurance in horsemanship, calling as it does for speed, jumping ability, stamina and obedience in the horse, and all-round knowledge, ability and versatility on the part of the rider, with supreme fitness of both. Known also as combined training, eventing combines three different equestrian disciplines – dressage, cross-country riding, including steeplechasing and jumping natural fences, and show-jumping. In the bigger and international events, these three phases are held over three days with stringent veterinary checks held throughout to make sure the horse is fit enough to continue.

Eventing has its origins way back in the cavalry training of centuries ago, but as a sport, it is a real newcomer. It owes something to the long distance military "endurance" ride popular as training in the eighteenth century for the French, German, Swedish and American cavalries. These rides could be anything from about 18 miles (29 km) to 450 miles (720 km); there may have been no jumping, but there was certainly an emphasis on endurance!

With this background it is not surprising that originally the army competed exclusively, and it is a sport in which army officers have repeatedly excelled. Early competitions at the beginning of this century were held by the French (the Championnat du Cheval d'Armes was held as a military exercise), the Swedish military, the Belgians and the Swiss. Even the Indian army organized such an event.

By 1912, eventing was sufficiently recognized to be included in the Olympics, with ten nations competing, but it did not really begin to progress in leaps and bounds in the popularity stakes until after World War II, at which time more and more civilians began to take part. The staging of the event by the Duke of Beaufort at his home in Badminton, Gloucestershire as a training ground for the 1952 Olympics established it as a major sport in England. This venue, originally intended to be the home for three competitions only (in 1949, 1950 and 1951), has become wholly synonymous with eventing. Most "horse-orientated" countries of the world today stage three-day events, many as international competitions; these include the USA, West Germany, Italy, Switzerland, Belgium, Holland, Ireland, France, Poland and the USSR.

Dressage, in its literal sense, means the training or schooling of a horse in order to make him supple, obedient and a pleasure to ride. The word comes from the French verb *dresser*, used to describe the training of a riding or harness horse, as distinct from *entrainer*, which means the training of a racehorse. Nowadays, we tend to think of dressage as the more advanced training of a riding horse; certainly a "dressage horse" – one trained to compete exclusively in dressage competitions – is generally schooled in more advanced and fluid paces than most ordinary leisure horses.

Dressage competitions are graded according to ability, ranging from the quite elementary preliminary grade to the highly advanced Grand Prix – a standard few horses attain. At all levels the horse is expected to be obedient, supple and light as he progresses through various movements performed at walk, trot and canter. The more advanced competitions call for more advanced school movements – changes of leg at the canter at every stride, half-pass, counter canter (cantering with the off-side foreleg leading to the left and vice versa), piaffe and passage. None of these movements is in itself intrinsically difficult to perform; the important factor is that they must all be executed with precision and fluent grace, so that each must appear to flow effortlessly into the next. Dressage is a sport in which horsemen from the continent of Europe, particularly the West Germans and Swiss, with their tradition of great riding schools, have always excelled.

Left and insert: The cross-country course is the most grueling part of a three-day event. Horse and rider are required to jump a number of spectacular, solid obstacles on the three- to four-mile course.

Right: The first part of a three-day event is the dressage phase. America's Bruce Davidson and J. J. Babu are seen here performing a movement in extended trot.

Driving

Driving is another ancient sport, one that perhaps saw a wane in popularity when the automobile made it a less-practiced skill but equally one that has resurfaced in recent years. It is both a leisure-time sport – Driving Societies and Organizations in different countries organize numbers of rallies and outings for their members – and a competitive sport, although one that does not currently have a place in the Olympics. Competitors in the driving world have to seek their titles at the World and European championships.

As with most competitive sports there are lots of different classes for driving enthusiasts ranging from competitions for horses in single harness to pairs, tandems and up to four- and six-in-hands. In Europe, it is possible to see teams of up to twelve horses pulling one conveyance. Probably, however, the most popular competition for both spectators and participators is that of *combined driving*.

This is the driving equivalent of the ridden three-day event; competitors perform tests over three days beginning with a presentation and dressage test on the first day, followed by a marathon cross-country course on the second and an obstacle driving course on the third. The presentation phase is judged on the turnout of horses, drivers and grooms and vehicle, while the dressage test involves performing a test of set movements around a marked-out arena.

In the cross-country, teams travel around a rugged course that will certainly take them through water, and which has to be completed within a set time – in fact certain sections of the course must be taken at a given pace and penalties are awarded if that pace is broken. Like the cross-country course of a three-day event, this is an exhausting exercise for driver and horses, demanding precision, stamina and fitness. As with the show-jumping phase of an event, the obstacle phase on the third day tests the horses' suppleness and fitness after the previous day's exertion. The team is required to weave around a course involving tight turns and narrow passages. Exacting and grueling the competition may be, but it is certainly one which is gaining a bigger entry each year.

Below: Combined driving is the equivalent of the ridden three-day event. This shows a team on the cross-country course.

Right: The two-day 75-mile Golden Horseshoe Ride across Exmoor is the most famous endurance ride in Britain.

Endurance riding

Endurance or long-distance riding is a sport that is particularly popular in the USA and Australia, and one in which the competitive element is more against oneself than against other horses and riders. This is because the aim is always to complete the course without over-stretching the horse, rather than to do so in the fastest possible time. It is an amazingly demanding sport; to get horse and rider fit to complete such a ride – which can be 100 miles (160 km) long – particularly if the distance is to be covered in one day, requires a toughness of body and mind achieved through rigorous training. The mental and physical stress of this must never be underestimated; endurance riding is certainly no "easy-option" sport.

Among the most famous of the American endurance rides is the Tevis Cup – a one day, 100-mile (160 km) ride held in the Sierra Nevada in California. It is generally held at the end of July or the beginning of August and awards are given to the horse that completes in the fastest time and in the best condition. Horse and rider have to take six compulsory stops, three of one hour each and three of 15 minutes, throughout the 24 hours, and they are subjected to

regular veterinarian tests before, during and after the ride. Awards are not given until the day following the ride so that the horses' condition subsequent to the ride can be checked. Numbers of other endurance rides are staged in different places in the United States, ranging from 50 to 100 miles (80 to 160 km). Some rides are staged over a three-day period; all are over difficult terrain with temperatures that may vary between below freezing at night to 100°F by midday.

Australia's most famous ride, held annually since 1966, is the 100-mile (160 km) Quilty Ride held across the rough ground of the Blue Mountains to the west of Sydney. In Great Britain, the most famous ride for endurance riders is the 75-mile (120 km) Golden Horseshoe that is held over two days across Exmoor in the south-west of the country. Riders have to complete 50 miles (80 km) on the first day, and then, if their horses pass the veterinarian tests, they complete the final 25 miles (40 km) on the second day. In all countries where endurance rides are held, horses with a high percentage of Arab blood consistently excel; an ancestry of centuries of harsh desert conditions still appears to produce an unrivaled degree of stamina in these horses.

Polo

Polo is the fastest team game in the world. While it undoubtedly developed in India and was introduced to the Western world by the English in the nineteenth century, it is possible that the game actually originated in Persia some 2500 years ago. First played in England in 1868 and in America in 1883, these two countries began to compete with one another in 1886 when the Anglo-American Westchester Trophy was first played. Today polo is a game that has a worldwide following and it is played in many countries. It found particular favor in South America, and Argentina has been one of the most successful countries to produce ponies that excel at the sport. (A polo "pony" can stand up to 15.2 h.h. but is still referred to as a pony.)

Polo is played between two teams of four players on a ground that measures 300 x 200 yds (274 x 182 meters) with a goal post at either end. The aim is to score goals by hitting the ball (with a specially designed mallet) through the goal posts. Play is carried out at a virtually continuous gallop in which the ponies are constantly being asked to halt and turn. So physically demanding is this that although a game will last for less than one hour, matches are split into periods, known as chukkas, of an average of just seven minutes each and each pony only plays in two chukkas during a game.

Showing

Showing is often included under an umbrella heading of "competitive equestrian sports", although one perhaps does not think of the show horse as a sports horse in the same way as some of the horses looked at in this chapter. However, there is no denying the popularity of the world of showing, and it is a field in which the myriad categories of classes provide opportunities for many different types of horses and of riders.

American horse shows have show classes for their own specific breeds and types, and these are further divided for three different styles of riding – the hunt seat, stock seat and saddle seat. As a general ruling, the southern states concentrate on the saddle seat, the western states on the stock seat and the remaining areas on the hunt seat, but it would not be unusual to find classes for the different styles at shows all over the country.

Below: Numerous show classes exist for horses and ponies. At this British show a class is in progress for children's riding ponies, groomed to look their best.

Right: Polo is the fastest game in the horse world. Developed in India, it is a game with worldwide popularity especially in Argentina, which produces top-class polo ponies.

Hunter classes, which are generally divided into pony, junior, green, working and conformation categories are shown in the hunt seat as might be expected, and all are required to jump in their showing classes. Arabian horses are mainly shown in the saddle and stock seats, while Western breeds are obviously shown in the stock seat. Most shows include competitions for pleasure horses, and these can be shown under all seats – those shown in saddle seat being expected to produce more impulsion than in the hunt seat, and those shown in the stock seat being asked to perform on a loose rein.

These horses are judged on performance, manners, conformation and suitability to the rider; Saddlebreds and Tennessee Walking Horses are often shown in pleasure horse classes. Equitation classes are popular and exhibitors may compete in both hunt and saddle seats. Classes in Western horse categories include those for cutting horses, stock horses and trail horses, and there are some spectacular sights as riders and horses parade in their finest clothes and tack.

In the larger shows in Britain there are showing classes for hunters, hacks, children's riding and show ponies, cobs, Arabians and the Mountain and Moorland pony breeds. All sizes and many shapes of horses and pony are catered for as there are classes for different grades – from novice to open – and different heights. In most showing classes, the horses and ponies are put through their paces in front of the judges, who will place them in order of preference after riding them themselves (in the case of horses) and judging them "stripped-out" (without a saddle). Of all "show" horses and ponies, it is only the working hunters in each category that are expected to jump.

The world of showing is as keenly competitive as any other and requires a great degree of dedication and skill on the part of rider and trainer. Horses have to look their very best, conditioned and groomed to perfection, and must be able to perform faultlessly in front of the judges. For a child whose pony may not be up to the show standard of the top ones in terms of looks and performance, there are countless small shows and gymkhanas (particularly in England) where they can take part in best rider classes and the ever-popular gymkhana games.

Individual National Sports

Many countries have their own individual sports which have been played in fierce competition, often for centuries, and which could be said to be part of a national heritage. The "gauchos" of South America, for example, play Pato – a game faintly reminiscent of a sort of "horseback rugby". Once played with a live duck, happily now substituted with an oval-shaped object with grips by which it can be held, the idea is that players should score goals by placing this in a net positioned at either end of the field. The game, as might be imagined, is carried out at a gallop, with riders retrieving the "ball" from the ground by leaning right out of the saddle.

Bullfighting is an often bloody sport which produces revulsion in many but is nevertheless still as popular as ever in those countries that have practiced it for hundreds of years. Most regularly performed in Spain and Portugal, it certainly calls for a high degree of skill in horsemanship.

Rodeo riding is also included in the world of competitive equestrian sports, and colorful rodeos with their traditional events of bronco riding, calf-roping and so on are held in North America, Canada and Australia. Canada's famous Calgary Stampede is considered to be one of the world's top attractions and spectators can watch the competitions of steer wrestling and Brahma bull riding as well as the more traditional events here. The famous chuck-wagon race can be seen at Calgary, too, the thrills and spills of which never fail to delight spectators – and the hard-driving participants.

Above: Steer-wrestling is one of the attractions at Canada's famous Calgary Stampede, considered to be one of the world's top events.

Right: The famous chuck-wagon race can also be seen at the Calgary Stampede. The colorful wagons and the thrills and spills never fail to delight the crowd.

Left: Rodeo-riding is a popular event in North America and Canada, and the colorful displays include bronco-riding, calf-roping, steer-wrestling and even Brahma bull-riding.

It was every show-jumper's dream. Virginia resident Joe Fargis had already ridden his great mare, Touch of Class, to a double clear round, leading the United States to victory in the Team Championship at the Los Angeles Olympic Games. Now he came into the arena for a jump-off for the individual gold medal, last to go and knowing that he could knock a fence down and still win. From the way Touch of Class had been jumping any error seemed unlikely.

The stadium at Santa Anita racecourse was packed and although it was a hot, airless day with the San Gabriel mountains towering behind through a haze of smog, every person there felt only the excitement. The equestrian events had been a tremendous success for the home team, and now Fargis and his former racehorse had the chance to put a golden finishing touch. As they cleared each fence, cheering burst irrepressibly from the crowd, building to a crescendo as they turned into the final double. It was here, in the second round, that Touch of Class had made her only mistake of the Games. This time, she was well clear, and the title was won.

Joe Fargis and Touch of Class had tied for first after the first round, their faultless circuit matched only by Britain's Michael Whitaker with Overton Amanda. In the second round, Amanda had reverted to her old aversion to water ditches – the second and third parts of a big treble combination – and Conrad Homfeld, Fargis' team-mate and business partner in their Petersfield, Va., stable, had the only clear round on his Trakehner stallion, Abdullah. When Touch of Class nudged off the last pole, the two were equal and had to jump off. Going first, however, Abdullah left the way open when he hit two fences.

These 1984 Olympic Games were the first in which the United States had won the team show jumping,

and only their second individual gold at the sport. The indomitable Bill Steinkraus had been the previous winner on Snowbound in Mexico 1968. He and Hungarian-born Bert de Nemethy have, more than anyone else, been responsible for the improving of standards of riding and training in the States that produced this dual success.

Getting the course right

De Nemethy, who had been chosen for the Hungarian Olympic squad in the 1940 Olympics (canceled because of World War II) emigrated to the United States after the war. He was appointed official coach to the United States Equestrian Team's Prix des Nations squad in 1955, a position he held until 1983. Throughout those years, during many of which Steinkraus was the riding captain of the team, de Nemethy produced generations of stylish, effective riders, and it is perhaps no mere coincidence that most of them rode Thoroughbreds, often "cast-offs" from the racetrack, like Touch of Class. After his retirement as coach, de Nemethy was appointed show jumping course builder for the Los Angeles Games. He made it clear from the beginning that he was going to change the pattern into which he felt the Olympics and World Championships had slipped.

The trend had become increasingly one of relying on the sheer size of fences to produce results, making them ever bigger. This policy gives the advantage to those horses with tremendous jumping power, such as the German and Dutch breeds, often at the expense of agility. Steinkraus, after he had retired from competition, said at one World Championships, "Courses like this will just make riders go home and ask themselves not how they can improve their riding, but how they can find the money to buy a better horse."

Left: Joe Fargis and Touch of Class, members of the US gold-medal-winning show-jumping team at the Los Angeles Olympics in 1984. Both the team and the individual gold medals went to the States.

Right: A competitor in the Munich Olympic Games of 1972 clears the parallel poles in fine style, part of the superb show-jumping course.

Harvey Smith, former British Olympic rider and now one of the top professionals, whose son Steven was in the British team in Los Angeles, echoed his sentiments when he commented, "If a mile runner goes to the Olympics, they don't ask him to run a mile and a quarter: but show jumpers are expected to tackle fences much bigger than in their normal competitions".

At Santa Anita, Bert de Nemethy faced the problem and proved the point. He wanted to build a course for the best-trained horses and the most experienced, skillful riders, not just for puissance horses. He achieved that ambition in a style that won him the applause of all the riders and officials involved, producing enthralling competitions without stretching the horses to, or even beyond, their limits. That the winners were from the United States was incidental.

In Montreal, 1976, the last previous true Olympic equestrian competition (most Federations outside Eastern Europe boycotted the competitions in Moscow), the course for the individual competition was so demanding that neither the winner, Alwin Schockemöhle's Warwick Rex, nor any of the three who jumped off for the silver and bronze medals – Michel Vaillancourt's Branch County (Canada), François Mathy's Gai Luron (Belgium) and Debbie Johnsey's Moxy (Great Britain) ever really excelled again. Yet only a couple of months after winning her Olympic golds, Touch of Class proved her well-being by triumphing in World Cup competitions on the indoor Fall circuit.

In the team competition, also, the 1984 scores alone show that the courses were much more in line with the usual run of high-class Prix des Nations, instead of being massive "freak" courses. The United States won with a total of twelve faults, and because they were in an unbeatable position their last rider, Melanie Smith, with Calypso, did not even need to jump a second time. If they had, and had repeated their faultless first circuit, the total would have been just *four* faults. Compare this with Montreal, where the winning total was 40; Munich, 32; and Mexico, a massive 102.75 faults for the gold-medal Canadians.

Left: The individual gold-medal-winner at the Montreal Olympics in 1978, Alwin Schockemöhle and Warwick Rex. He won, despite not going clear on the demanding course.

Living legends

When Canada claimed this success in 1976, she was only the second non-European country to win an Olympic team gold. Mexico, at London in 1948, was the first. In between, and following Great Britain's success in 1952 led by the legendary Harry Llewellyn and Foxhunter, Olympic show-jumping had been dominated by the Germans. They were victorious in Stockholm, 1956, Rome, 1960, Tokyo, 1964 and on home ground in Munich, 1972. No doubt there was something of a "chicken-and-egg" situation in the sport at the top level; because the courses were big, German horses, better suited to them than most of their rivals, did well; and because these horses were so successful they became increasingly popular among riders and owners of other nations, who were then more disposed to jumping large-fence courses.

The names of some of the horses that took the titles in those days are now legendary – and none more so than Hans Gunter Winkler's Halla. This mare won the Individual and Team Gold in 1956, and a Team Gold four years later, as well as a couple of World Championships. Halla went to stud after she retired from jumping and produced several foals, but none could quite match up to her fantastic ability.

Germany's breeding societies keep better records than most, and so are able to "channel" stallions and mares in the right direction for success. In Holland, too, there is a strict stallion control. In recent years, France has produced consistently good types; the Selle

Français or French saddle horse (see page 40) is a first-rate all-rounder, and also accounts for some outstanding show jumpers. Notable are the stallions Galoubet – now retired from competition and at stud in the United States – and I Love You, on which Norman dello Joio won the World Cup in 1983 and tied for second in 1984.

In Britain and Ireland the traditional aim has been to breed horses for hunting, which means that, above all, they have to be good across country; hence Britain's long run of success in three-day events. In general, the horses have been less suitable for the mammoth Olympic and championship show-jumping courses, but if the trend in course-building set by de Nemethy is continued, they could yet come back into their own.

Throughout history, however, show-jumping horses have come in all shapes and sizes. There was the one-eyed Arete, on which Humberto Mariles of Mexico won individual and team gold medals in London in 1948, and more recently little Stroller, which, with Marion Coakes in the saddle, was probably the most popular horse in Britain. In fact, Stroller was only a pony – Marion rode him in junior competitions – but it was when she grew too old for these, and took him into adult international competitions over bigger obstacles, that he showed his real prowess. Together they won the Women's World Championship, the British Jumping Derby at Hickstead and took an astonishing silver medal in Mexico, behind Bill Steinkraus and Snowbound.

Right: Norman Dello Joio World Cup Winner in 1983 on I Love You, seen here competing in England on Allegro. I Love You became one of France's top Selle Français breeding stallions.

Left: In the water at the Montreal Olympics is the individual three-day-event gold medallist, American Edmund Coffin and Bally-Cor. The speed and endurance test is the most crucial part of any three-day event.

The Eventers

The tests in the sport of eventing are dressage, speed-and-endurance and show-jumping – and none of the contestants ever emerges with a clean sheet at the end of the three days' exhausting sport.

Dressage, held on the first day, is full of hazards. The horse must be totally obedient to his rider's every instruction in order to give a smooth, calm performance, yet he must be supremely fit and on his toes for the next day's speed-and-endurance test. Horses that are in such top form are never easy to control.

The second day's event, the speed-and-endurance, is divided into four phases – roads and tracks, steeplechase, roads and tracks again and, finally, the cross-country jumping course. At international level, this means a total of around 15 miles (24 kilometers) of strictly regulated and timed work, ending in a fast ride over some 30 or so jumps of widely differing types and including a few which are dreaded by even the best riders. It is one of the most grueling tests for a sportsman or woman.

The show-jumping phase on day three is a searching test for horses that have given their all the previous day, as well as for riders who will also certainly be feeling the strain of lengthy, demanding competition.

Because the crucial part of any three-day event is the second phase, the speed-and-endurance, the horse needs to be able to gallop over some distance as well as jump, and he must have the stamina to keep up the pace to the bitter end. The dressage, which precedes this part of the competition, has so improved in standard over the last few years that no one who wants to have a chance for a medal can afford to be below standard in this discipline. The final phase of show-jumping, over a smaller course than for the jumping specialists, is designed to prove that the horse is still fit, supple and obedient.

After the first two phases at the 1984 Olympics, it looked as though the United States might capture a double gold in this sport too, for they were leading the team competition, and Karen Stives, with the Irish-bred Ben Arthur, was ahead individually. In both categories, however, their lead was much smaller than in the show-jumping competition, and although they just managed to maintain it in the teams, Karen was overtaken in the final phase by Mark Todd of New Zealand, on Charisma.

Only one event horse in Olympic history has won two Individual gold medals and that is the Dutch-entered Marcroix, ridden to victory in 1928 in Amsterdam and again four years later (when the Olympics were first held in Los Angeles) by Charles Pahud de Mortanges, a Lieutenant in the Dutch Hussars. Marcroix was, in fact, not Dutch but French, by an English Thoroughbred sire, Marsan. Mortanges bought him in France just before the 1928 Games, and won in a desperately tight finish from his team-mate Gerard de Kruyff on Va-t-en. Los Angeles was a much

more difficult place to get to in 1932 than in 1984 when horses could be "jetted-in" with ease, and as a result only four teams took part in the three-day event. The Dutch went all the way by boat. The journey took them a month. A walking machine was rigged up on the deck to keep the horses reasonably fit, so that when they landed in California they were ready to go straight into strong work. It paid off, for they finished second to the United States.

Once more, Marcroix won by only a whisper. In Amsterdam, his margin had been just 2.56 points in nearly 2,000; now he had 1,813.83 to the 1,811 of Earl

Thomson of the United States on Jenny Camp, and that included ten penalties for Jenny Camp when a hind foot slid back into the water jump in the show-jumping phase after she had landed.

If Charles Mortanges and Marcroix were blessed by fate, Earl Thomson and Jenny Camp were certainly frowned upon. Four years later in Berlin, during the Games that were Hitler's "showcase", they came in second again, after being penalized for a refusal which also cost them time, even though they had been stopped by an official because there was a rider in a ditch in front of them. And then Stubbendor, who

Above: America's Karen Stives with the Irish-bred Ben Arthur, members of the winning three-day event team in the 1984 Olympics, pictured in top form in England in 1983.

won for Germany on Nurmi, failed to make the weight, but was not disqualified. It would have taken a brave offical to dismiss a home rider in Nazi days.

In 1936 the United States was still without its first Olympic eventing gold but was to remedy this when the Games were resumed after World War II in London in 1948, when Earl Thomson rode on the winning US team.

Badminton

It was as a result of the 1948 Olympic three-day event that the Duke of Beaufort, feeling that here was a sport at which the British could do well, decided to stage an annual event at his estate at Badminton in England's rolling west country. He thus began what is generally agreed to be the most prestigious annual three-day event in the world. The Duke of Beaufort's aim was to give the British the experience they needed to take on the best from overseas, and his training-ground paid magnificent dividends.

The first golden reward came at Stockholm in 1956, through a team that included Colonel Frank Weldon. This doyen of the sport has for many years been the director, organizer and course designer at Badminton, always aiming to maintain that first principal of keeping British horses and riders at the top level of international competition. The British had a tremendous run of success in the late 1960s and early 1970s, winning the team gold in Mexico, and the team and individual golds in Munich. The latter was taken by Richard Meade on Laurieston and, in that same period, he also won one World and three European championships.

Mary Gordon-Watson took the 1969 European and 1970 World individual titles, as well as being a member of the winning teams those years, on one of the sport's greatest horses, Cornishman V. This duo were also on the team that won in Munich, finishing fourth individually. Richard Meade rode Cornishman in Mexico, again in the winning team and coming in fourth in the individual. As his name implies, this horse was bred in Cornwall and when Mary's father went to buy him his first action was to put that distinguished horseman on the ground. He was never an easy ride, but no cross-country fence in the world proved too much for him.

Badminton also showed eventing fans in the Northern Hemisphere the talent of New Zealand dairy farmer Mark Todd. He won at Badminton in 1980 on Southern Comfort, and returned four years later with Charisma on his way to Olympic glory, to beat all but the World Champion – Lucinda Green.

Charisma, who started his competitive career as a Pony Club horse, is small for an eventer, and the lanky Todd emphasized the horse's lack of height, but they made a fine team, equally proficient in all three phases.

Below: Edward Pybus on Good News clearing the Elephant Trap at Badminton, England, a tough cross-country fence at this most prestigious annual three-day event.

Ben Arthur

In eventing as in show-jumping the United States owes much of its present strength to a European trainer, former French Olympic rider Jack le Goff. The 1984 Games marked for him the end of a decade as the US National team coach, although he continues to find and train young riders. The strength of the home side was evident right from the start in 1984; Bruce Davidson, the only man ever to have won two World titles, was second after the dressage, ahead of Karen Stives with Ben Arthur. The Irish-bred Ben Arthur used to be ridden by New Zealander Mary Hamilton, but at the 1982 World Championships Miss Stives' mother insisted that she get "first refusal" on the horse

Above: Individual silver medallist at Los Angeles in 1984, Karen Stives and Ben Arthur competing in the final show-jumping phase of the three-day event.

if the owner wanted to sell him. Not surprisingly, Karen is on record as saying, "I'm sure glad she did."

Dressage judging is always a matter of personal opinion, and there was more argument about the marks given to Ben Arthur than any other major contender in 1984. Even le Goff the coach said later that he had expected the horse to get around 55 penalty points, instead of the 49.2 that he was given. That difference would have put Karen out of the individual medals, and given the team gold to Britain.

Cross-country

There had been much fear beforehand that the speed-and-endurance phase of the event would be run in torrid heat, taking too much out of the horses, as had happened when the World Championships were held at Lexington, Kentucky, in 1978. To guard against this it was held 120 miles (193 kilometers) south of Los Angeles, at Fairbanks Ranch where the sea breeze made conditions perfect. Course-builder Neil Ayer had constructed a gem for the cross-country, even though he had to put it in the confines of a golf course.

Just like de Nemethy's show-jumping courses, Ayer's cross-country asked all the questions that needed to be answered without subjecting the horses to undue strain. Time proved the essential ingredient, and only four competitors completed the course within the time allowed – Ben Arthur, Charisma, Lucinda Green with Regal Realm, and Italy's Marina Sciochetti on Master Hunt. Britain's Ginny Holgate (eventually to take the bronze with Priceless) was only a second too slow.

The sloping terrain made unusual demands upon the horses, and after the trail-blazing round of US team captain Mike Plumb – in his sixth Olympics, a record for any American – Ben Arthur wore special studs to stop him from slipping. As a result the big, long-striding horse "went round the turns like a ski-racer", said a delighted Karen Stives.

At the end of the day Karen and Ben Arthur were ahead, but by less than the cost of one show-jumping mistake, from Charisma, with Ginny Holgate and Priceless ready to take advantage of any mistakes by the two leaders. Ben Arthur made just one error, at the middle of the treble, but Charisma was clear, so the two reversed their standings. Priceless was clear, but still third. This was the first time New Zealand had had a full team in an Olympic three-day event, and the first time a woman had taken an individual medal. Another woman rider, Torrance Fleischmann, with Finvarra, had the only clear show-jumping round for the US team. It proved a vital one, too, as it left them 3.2 points ahead of Britain, who had risen from fourth at the end of the dressage, but could not quite make up the deficit.

Below: Lucinda Green on Regal Realm: one of only four to complete the Los Angeles cross-country in the time allowed.

Right: One of the German competitors, Klaus Erhorn on Fair Lady, seen here at the water obstacle in Los Angeles.

The masters of dressage

Olympic Grand Prix dressage is in quite a different league from that demanded in eventing. The movements are much more complex, including those of piaffes, pirouettes and passages that would never be expected of an event horse. Probably the biggest certainty of the entire 1984 Olympic Games was that the West Germans would win the team dressage, and so they did, although perhaps, with the exception of Reiner Klimke and Ahlerich – who went on also to take the individual title – not quite as impressively as expected. This brought Dr. Klimke's score of Olympic gold medals to five, equaling the record in equestrian events set by his distinguished show-jumping compatriot, Hans Gunter Winkler.

Training a Grand Prix dressage horse takes at least four years, and although Dr. Klimke, a practicing lawyer, is able to work with his horses only in his spare time, it is a measure of his dedication and ability that he has won Olympic gold medals on three different horses. Modestly, he said afterwards that Dux, the horse he rode in the winning teams in Tokyo and Mexico, where he was also third individually," . . . was as good a horse as Ahlerich, but I was not".

The emotion and relief that Dr. Klimke clearly felt in at last achieving his major goal in 1984 was transmitted to the crowd, most of whom had never seen a dressage test of this kind before the Games. Unlike the afficionados of Aachen, that Mecca of dressage, they may not, perhaps, have appreciated the finer points of the performance, but were only too well aware that they were witnessing a superb display by a true champion.

Germany has won every team dressage since the 1964 Tokyo Olympics except, ironically, in Munich when they were second to a Soviet team which brought a touch of balletic brilliance to the arena (and also, of course, in Moscow in 1980). The individual gold in Moscow went to Austria's former European champion, Elisabeth Theurer on Mon Chéri.

At first the German dressage dominance produced a somewhat "heavy" approach in which accuracy was really the sole criterion. Dr. Klimke, however, without sacrificing accuracy in the least, produced tests which were also lively and exciting to watch. He reveled in the electric atmosphere of the crowded Santa Anita stadium and Ahlerich responded most nobly. It was a victory crowning a series of successes by Dr. Klimke that was in the finest tradition of the modern Olympics.

Below: Individual and team dressage gold medallist at Los Angeles, Dr. Reiner Klimke and Ahlerich from West Germany. This brought Dr. Klimke's total of Olympic gold medals to five.

Right: Mark Todd and Charisma from New Zealand, who took the individual gold medal in the three-day event at Los Angeles and was the first New Zealander to win at Badminton.

Joe Fargis, born April 2, 1948; from Petersburg Virginia, where he runs a stable in partnership with Conrad Homfeld. He was a member of the show jumping team that won the Pan American Games gold medal in 1975 and on the US team for 14 years. Winner of individual and team show-jumping gold medals in Los Angeles in 1984, he also topped the US East Coast league in the World Cup in the same year.

Otto Hofer, born June 28, 1944; a salesman from Schaan, whose previous best performance had been a team bronze in the 1983 European dressage championships, surprised himself as much as anyone when, riding Limandus, he led the Swiss team to take the silver behind West Germany, and then the individual bronze in Los Angeles, his first Olympic Games.

Heidi Robbiana, born October 27, 1950; from Brusata, Switzerland. Rode in her first Nations Cup in 1982 and the following season was a member of the Swiss team that won the European Championship, in which she was eighth individually. Won the Individual bronze in Los Angeles show-jumping after a jump-off, and a member of the team that finished fifth.

Conrad Homfeld, born December 25, 1951; from Petersburg Virginia. Runs a stable in partnership with Joe Fargis and was a member of the team that finished third in the 1978 world show-jumping championships, when he was twelfth individually. Won the World Cup final in Baltimore in 1980 and in Berlin in 1985; a member of the gold medal team, and second individually in the Los Angeles Olympics.

Mark Todd, born March 1, 1956; from Cambridge, New Zealand, but based for much of the time in England. A dairy farmer by profession but presently concentrating on his riding, he was the first competitor from New Zealand to win a major three-day event in the Northern Hemisphere at Badminton, 1980, on Southern Comfort. Returned with Charisma to be second at Badminton, 1984, en route to Los Angeles where they won the three-day event. The New Zealand team, in their first Olympics, was sixth.

Virginia Holgate, born February 2, 1955; lives at Badminton, Gloucestershire. Won the European Junior three-day event Championship in 1973 and pre-Olympic event in Montreal, 1975, but two years later broke her arm so badly, in more than twenty places, in a riding fall, that there were fears it might have to be amputated. Thankfully, she recovered sufficiently to make her senior team debut in the 1981 European Championships, leading them to victory, as she did in the World Team Championship in 1982. A member of the European silver medal team in 1983; and took team silver and individual bronze in Los Angeles, first and third at Badminton 1985.

Anne Grethe Jensen, who has to fit in her riding with her work as a secretary, was unimpressed when her husband, who is also her trainer, and a former Danish Olympic dressage rider, bought the then-ungainly Marzog as a six-year-old. But the transformation they have brought resulted in two sensations in 1983, first when they beat Reiner Klimke and Ahlerich in the Grand Prix in the Indoor show in Dortmund, in the Spring, and again when they confirmed that form for her to become the first Danish rider to win the European Championship, in Aachen. Mrs Jensen, in her first Olympics, was somewhat nervous in Los Angeles, and she and her 11-year-old Marzog never threatened to beat Ahlerich, but were worthy silver medalists. Their team finished fifth.

Reiner Klimke, born January 14, 1936; from Munster. A practicing lawyer, he started his riding career in dressage, but then switched to three-day events. Member of the team that won the European Championship at Harewood, Yorkshire, in 1959, National Champion in 1960 and rode in Olympic Games in Rome that year, finishing 16th. Then returned to dressage: was World Champion in 1974 and 1982, European Champion 1967 and 1973; member of the Olympic gold medal teams in 1964, 1968, both with Dux, in 1976 with Mehmed, and in 1984 with Ahlerich.

Karen Stives, born November 3, 1950; from Dover, Massachusetts. Has ridden since a child, showing ponies and junior hunters, and proved herself proficient at dressage and show-jumping before concentrating on three-day events. Candidate for USET Dressage squad for Pan American Games in 1979. Rode in the "Olympic Susbstitute" event at Fontainebleu, 1980, as an individual, finishing 34th. Member of winning team and second individually in Los Angeles Olympic three-day event.

Right: Britain's Virginia Holgate and Priceless, who were members of the three-day event silver-medal-winning team as well as winning the individual bronze at Los Angeles.

Left: Melanie Smith and Calypso, who produced a faultless clear round to help the US team take the gold medal for show-jumping at the 1984 Los Angeles Olympics.

Melanie Smith on Calypso clears the Olympic logo with great panache.

1948 London

Dressage	Individual:	H Moser, Switzerland, on Hummer
	Team:	France
Show-Jumping	Individual:	H Mariles Cortés, Mexico, on Arete
	Team:	Mexico
3-Day Event	Individual:	B Chevallier, France, on Aiglonne
	Team:	USA

1952 Helsinki

Dressage	Individual:	H Saint Cyr, Sweden, on Master Rufus
	Team:	Sweden
Show-Jumping	Individual:	P J d'Oriola, France, on Ali Baba
	Team:	Great Britain
3-Day Event	Individual:	H von Blixen-Finecke, Sweden, on Jubal
	Team:	Sweden

1956 Stockholm

Dressage	Individual:	H Saint Cyr, Sweden, on Juli XXX
	Team:	Sweden
Show-Jumping	Individual:	H G Winkler, Germany, on Halla
	Team:	Germany
3-Day Event	Individual:	P Kastenman, Sweden, on Illuster
	Team:	Great Britain

1960 Rome

Dressage	Individual:	S Filatov, USSR, on Absent
	Team:	—
Show-Jumping	Individual:	R d'Inzeo, Italy, on Posillipo
	Team:	Germany
3-Day Event	Individual:	L Morgan, Australia, on Salad Days
	Team:	Australia

1964 Tokyo

Dressage	Individual:	H Chammartin, Switzerland, on Woermann
	Team:	Germany
Show-Jumping	Individual:	P J d'Oriola, France, on Lutteur B
	Team:	Germany
3-Day Event	Individual:	M Checcoli, Italy, on Surbean
	Team:	Italy

1968 Mexico

Dressage	Individual:	I Kizimov, USSR, on Ikhor
	Team:	Germany
Show-Jumping	Individual:	W Steinkraus, USA, on Snowbound
	Team:	Canada
3-Day Event	Individual:	J Guyon, France, on Pitou
	Team:	Great Britain

1972 Munich

Dressage	Individual:	Mrs L Linsenhoff, Germany, on Piaff
	Team:	USSR
Show-Jumping	Individual:	G Mancinelli, Italy, on Ambassador
	Team:	Germany
3-Day Event	Individual:	R Meade, Great Britain, on Laurieston
	Team:	Great Britain

1976 Montreal

Dressage	Individual:	Miss C Stuckelberger, Switzerland, on Granat
	Team:	West Germany
Show-Jumping	Individual:	A Schockemöhle, Germany, on Warwick Rex
	Team:	France
3-Day Event	Individual:	E Coffin, USA, on Bally-Cor
	Team:	USA

1980 Moscow

Dressage	Individual:	Miss E Theurer, Austria, on Mon Chéri
	Team:	—
Show-Jumping	Individual:	J Kowalczyk, Poland, on Artemor
	Team:	USSR
3-Day Event	Individual:	F Roman, Italy, on Rossinan
	Team:	USSR

1980 'Substitute' Olympics (Goodwood, GB)

Dressage	Individual:	Miss C Stuckelberger, Switzerland, on Granat
	Team:	West Germany

(Rotterdam, Holland)

Show-Jumping	Individual:	H Simon, Austria, on Gladstone
	Team:	Canada

(Fontainebleau, France)

3-Day Event	Individual:	N Haagensen, Denmark, on Monaco
	Team:	France

1984 Los Angeles

Dressage	Individual:	R Klimke, Germany, on Ahlerich
	Team:	West Germany
Show-Jumping	Individual:	J Fargis, USA, on Touch of Class
	Team:	USA
3-Day Event	Individual:	M Todd, New Zealand, on Charisma
	Team:	USA

Lipizzaner mares and foals at the State Stud at Piber, in Austria. Each year only about eight to ten of the most suitable three-year-old stallions are selected for training in *haute école*.

THE SPANISH RIDING SCHOOL OF VIENNA

It is seven in the morning in Vienna's Reitschul-gasse, a quiet street just behind the Opera House. A few early morning commuters on their way to work in the city center are held up while a line of white horses is led across the road and through an archway into the massive "Winter School" building for their morning workout. Here they rehearse and train to become part of the world's most famous team of dressage horses.

Later in the day the school's great colonnaded riding hall is bathed in sparkling light from massive chandeliers, as the beautiful Lipizzaner stallions of the Spanish Riding School make their entrance, their riders in the traditional uniforms worn at the School since the eighteenth century. The riders doff their bicorne hats in salute to the magnificent portrait of the founder and, to the music of Bizet, begin the highlight of the show, the School Quadrille. Visitors watch enthralled as horses and riders demonstrate their skill in the art of equitation.

The first record of the Spanish Riding School in Vienna dates from 1565. At this time, however, it was merely an open riding area in the Imperial Palace gardens. Over the next 150 years several plans were drawn up for a new building, nothing of which materialized, and it was not until Austria and the Hapsburg Empire were at the height of their power that Emperor Charles VI planned the rebuilding of the Hofburg, the Imperial Palace, to include a Winter Riding School. The magnificent Baroque building was completed in 1735 and is decorated entirely in white, with two galleries supported by Corinthian columns, and lit entirely by three beautiful chandeliers.

Above: The School Quadrille being performed to the music of Bizet by eight horses and riders beneath the beautiful chandeliers in the Baroque riding hall.

At one end of the hall is the arched doorway through which the horses enter and leave and at the other, facing it, is the Imperial Box above which hangs the portrait of the founder, Charles VI. Above the portrait is a tablet bearing a Latin inscription detailing the aims of the school as ". . . to be used for the Instruction and Training of the Youth of the Nobility and for the Schooling of the Horses in Riding for Art and War", an aim more democratically translated today as being ". . . to safeguard the tradition of the classical art of riding and to convince today's riders of its value".

The School was opened by the Emperor in September 1735 and subsequently, a number of carousels, ceremonies, festivals, balls and exhibitions were held there in addition to the daily routines of training horses and riders.

The most spectacular carousel ever to take place at the School was that held in November 1814 to which Austria's Emperor Franz I sent invitations to all the Kings of Europe. Competitions for tilting at rings, "Moor-baiting", in which wooden heads of Turks erected on posts were "to be lopped off at one blow" by charging knights in full armor, and mock battles as well as knightly tournaments and quadrilles were arranged for the guests' benefit. The last carousel was held in the hall in 1894 after which the School was devoted exclusively to the training of horse and rider in *haute école*.

Above: This single riderless stallion shows his high degree of schooling in the long reins. His trainer is wearing traditional uniform dating from the eighteenth century.

Haute école

Haute école is the classical term used to describe the training of the horse in the extension of his natural paces, balance and ability until he is able to perform the most difficult exercises in perfect harmony. There are three stages of training. Initially, the horse must learn to go forward freely and calmly, and for the first few weeks the horses are allowed to run free in the arena under the watchful eye of the trainers. Work on the lunge is then started and continues for eight to ten weeks before the horse is introduced to a rider. During the first year the horse learns to carry himself under the rider and respond to the basic aids.

In the second year, training progresses to include the perfect execution of turns and circles at all paces. A degree of balanced collection in conjunction with increased impulsion will now be asked for and suppling exercises to increase the horse's flexibility at all gaits are introduced. In-hand work begins in preparation for teaching the horse piaffe – a high-stepping trot performed on the same spot, in which each leg appears to remain suspended for an instant.

In their third year, the horses are assigned to specific trainers for the first time, the most experienced trainer taking on the most promising horse. Lateral movements and collected paces now predominate and the piaffe, passage, flying changes and pirouette are taught. Work "between pillars" is also started during the third year if the horse is considered to be ready for this more vigorous training. The pillars are an unusual feature of training at the School, introduced some 400 years ago and still in use for the advanced training. They comprise two stout posts just over 6 ft (2 m) tall, driven into the ground about 5 feet (1.5 m) apart, and to which a special halter can be attached. The pillars teach respect for the whip (used only in the lightest manner) and help achieve a more "elevated" action.

The final stage of training involves the extreme collection and agility necessary to execute the jumps or "airs above the ground".

The three airs above the ground for which the Spanish Riding School is noted are the *levade*, the *courbette* and the *capriole*. All are developed from the piaffe. In the levade, the horse supports his weight on

deeply bent hindquarters and lifts his forehand off the ground with his forelegs drawn in, remaining motionless. The courbette is a similar movement to the levade but, having stood up on his hind legs, the horse then moves forward in a series of leaps on his hindlegs. The forelegs still do not touch the ground. The capriole is the most difficult and impressive of all the airs; in this the horse jumps with all four legs off the ground simultaneously and, while his body is horizontal in mid-air, he kicks out with his hindlegs before landing on all fours.

These movements, quite spectacular and even menacing when seen by an unmounted watcher, have their origins in the battlefields of history. A courbette could be used to intimidate enemy footsoldiers and a capriole (as well as the simpler pirouette) could often get a horse and rider out of a dangerous situation.

The airs are all taught initially at the Spanish Riding School and, depending how they are performed at this early stage, the trainer decides which of the airs will most suit his horse. Each horse specializes in one particular movement.

Above right: A display on the long reins. Note the pillars, introduced some 400 years ago and still in use for advanced training. They can be used, together with a special halter, to gain a more elevated action.

Right: The *Pas de Deux;* two senior riders perform their "ballet on horseback".

Left: The *levade*, one of the three "airs above the ground" for which the Spanish Riding School is famous, seen here performed at a rehearsal. These movements have their origin on the battlefields.

The stud

Traditionally, descendants of the Spanish horses used in processions since Caesar's day are the horses used at the Spanish School. In 1580, Archduke Charles of Austria founded a royal stud at Lipizza, near Trieste, where selective breeding of the Spanish-bred Andalusian horses ensured a constant supply of the best stallions to the new school. However, three times during the Napoleonic Wars the horses were forced to flee from Lipizza, the final time being in May 1809. They were not to return until 1815.

With the outbreak of the World War I the horses were again evacuated, the stud horses and young mares to Laxenburg near Vienna, and the rest of the mares and stallions to Kladrub. When the Hapsburg empire collapsed, Lipizza became part of Italy, and the Lipizzaners were divided equally between Italy and Austria, Austria's animals being taken to the stud farm at Piber in the coalmining region of Western Styria. Here, apart from a three-year evacuation to Bohemia in 1942, they have remained ever since.

The rescue by American General George Patton of the School's Lipizzaners from almost certain extinction during World War II is one of the most dramatic incidents in the history of the School. Without Patton's rapid action the Spanish Riding School might have been permanently closed. The horses had been evacuated to Czechoslovakia during the war and in the confusion in the spring of 1945 they, and several hundred allied prisoners of war, were in the path of the communist advance in the area. Patton gave permission for a task force to move men and horses. "Get them out. Make it fast," he signaled. The small town of Hostau, still behind German lines, was reached and it has been said, the reception was jubilant. Some 300 breeding Lipizzaners and around 900 other horses were found there and were now safe in the new American area of operations.

The six distinct strains of Lipizzaner horses at Piber today are descended from the following:
Pluto – a gray born in 1765 and brought from the Royal Danish Court Stud at Frederiksborg.
Conversano – A black Neapolitan born in 1767 and closely related to the Andalusian.
Favory – a dun Kladruber from Bohemia, born in 1779.
Neapolitano – A bay from Italy, born in 1790.
Siglavy – A gray Arab born in 1810.
Maestoso – A gray born in 1819 of Spanish ancestry.
Of the original 23 female lines only 14 have been preserved to the present day.

Below: Lipizzaner mares and foals at the State Stud at Piber. The foals are born black and only lighten with age. The occasional bays are not used for breeding.

Right: The School quadrille which ends the enthralling performance, a display of perfectly-controlled horsemanship at the stateliest indoor school in the world.

Although the School horses were originally of various colors – bays, duns, creams, blacks etc. – white horses were considered to be the most suitable color for "horses of the Emperor". Lipizzaners born at the stud today are born gray, brown or black and gradually change to white over (approximately) a five year period. The bays that sometimes appear are not used for breeding, although traditionally one bay stallion is kept at the School.

The selection of the stallions to be trained in *haute école* at the School takes place at Piber when the horses are three-and-a-half years old. Every Autumn, eight to ten of the most suitable ones are sent to Vienna where their training under the dedicated Riders of the School commences when the horses reach four years of age. The remaining animals and those whose training has shown them to be below standard are sold.

The mares at Piber are also schooled to go under saddle and later to draw a carriage, and when they are four or five years old, those with the best conformation and temperament are put in foal. The sires used are the stallions who have proved themselves to be outstanding in training at the School.

The Lipizzaner should stand between 15.1 h.h. to 16.2 h.h. and be compact, strong and muscular, particularly in the back and hindquarters. The neck is set high and the head is large, but well-shaped, frequently with a slight Roman nose. The tail is set high and the limbs placed squarely under the body with short cannon bones and big knees and hocks. Lieutenant Colonel Hubert Rudofsky, an early Director of the Piber Stud, writes, "Being of a practical medium size, the Lipizzaner is a very strong, durable, spirited horse, easy enough to maintain, very teachable, intelligent, and well behaved. Next to the primitive miniature horse, the Lipizzaners are the slowest horses in the world to mature, but they compensate by living to a very great age. Stallions that serve the Spanish Riding School as School horses and teachers for 20 or even 25 years are by no means rare". Many of them live to be 30 years old and more.

The only differences between the horses bred at Lipizza and Piber are the brand marks, the Piber bred stock having a P with the Austrian Imperial Crown above it branded on their left croup in addition to the L which is branded on their left cheek. The horses bred at Lipizza just have the L brand on the left cheek. In addition, the ancestral brand – a symbol denoting the dam's sire and the initial letter of the appropriate stallion line – is marked under the saddle, and the registration number in the stud book is branded on the right side of the back.

The performance

The object of the School is to maintain the classical art of horsemanship in its purest form and performances, comprising seven "acts", are given twice weekly. By tradition one bay or brown horse figures in the program in addition to the famous white stallions.

Accompanied by the music of Riedinger, Chopin, Mozart, Bizet and Boccherini, the first part comprises the exhibition of eight young ridden stallions who are just completing their first year of training. They perform the basic movements of walk, trot and canter with turns and circles. Four stallions who have finished their third year's training perform the next part, demonstrating the steps and movements of the classical school, which include the piaffe, the passage in which the horse trots – almost floats – forward with a similar moment of suspended extension between each stride; the pirouette, in which the forelegs describe a circle around the hindlegs which act as pivot, and flying changes of leg in single, double and triple strides.

The Pas de Deux follows in which two senior riders perform what could be called a "ballet" on horseback, before the work on the short hand-rein is performed from the ground between the pillars set in the center of

Above: Stallions who are just completing their first year of training. The first year is concerned with developing balance and control in the paces of walk, trot and canter.

the Hall. Next, a single riderless stallion shows his high degree of schooling in the long reins, and then comes the display of the famous airs above the ground, the most gifted of the stallions performing the levade, courbette and capriole. The program ends with the School Quadrille in which eight or twelve horses perform the classical movements in formation.

The Spanish Riding School is among the last remaining institutions where classical horsemanship is still practiced as a true art.

Left: Levade on the short hand rein. This young Lipizzaner stallion has not yet learned to support his weight on deeply bent hindquarters in the manner of the *haute école.*

Right: The early aim of the Spanish Riding School was "that it be used for the instruction and training of the youth of the Nobility", and "Riding for Art and War".

Glossary

Action – The manner in which a horse moves.

Aids – The signals whereby the rider communicates his wishes to the horse, i.e. his use of hands, legs, seat and voice.

Backed – Reference to the horse being mounted for the first time in its early training.

Balanced – A loose horse balances himself naturally but once mounted this balance is upset. A rider then has to sit and use the aids correctly to help the horse find his new balance.

Breastplate – A piece of equipment attached to the saddle to prevent it from slipping back.

Brushing – When the horse strikes the fore or hind leg with its opposite fore or hind leg, knocking the fetlock joint. The result of faulty action.

Cantle – The back of the saddle.

Cast – A horse, lying down in the stable and unable to rise without assistance (usually through lack of space or being too close to a wall) is said to be cast.

Carousel – A musical ride executed by a group of riders.

Cavesson – The simplest form of noseband. Also a specially constructed tough headcollar used in lunging.

Clenches – The pointed end of shoeing nails which protrude through the hoof after the horse has been shod.

Left: Examples of hard feed. Oats, barley, nuts are energy-producing feeds given to horses in work.

Above: Detail of a breast plate. This piece of equipment is used to prevent the saddle from slipping back and is often used by riders in hilly country.

Colt – Ungelded male horse under the age of four years.

Combined system – A horse stabled at night and turned out in the paddock during the day (or vice versa) is said to be kept on the combined system.

Concentrate feed – energy producing food, i.e. oats, nuts, barley etc., as opposed to grass, hay, bran etc.

Concussion – The result of fast work on hard roads producing heat and tenderness in the legs.

Counter Canter – A dressage movement in which the horse canters with the outer, rather than the usual inner, leg leading.

Crib-biting – A stable vice developed through boredom when the horse gets hold of the manger, door or any other projection with his teeth and sucks wind at the same time.

Cut-back head – A saddle with the tree cut away at the head to provide clearance for the withers.

Filly – Female horse under four years old.

Flying change – A school movement involving a change of leading leg at the canter without a break into trot to strike off on the new lead.

Gelding – A castrated male horse.

Half-pass – A lateral movement used in schooling the horse to a fairly high standard, where the horse moves both sideways and forwards.

Haute école – Literally high school; the classic art of equitation, in accordance with traditions passed down by the great equestrian masters of the past.

Head carriage – The position of the horse's head.

h.h. – Hands high.

Impulsion – The urge to move forward, manifested by the energetic use of the hocks, in a controlled fashion as in the well-schooled horse.

Lateral movements – Sideways movements.

Manger – A container into which a horse's food is put.

Nut-cracker action – The squeezing action across the lower jaw brought about by a jointed snaffle bit.

One-sided – A horse that is more supple when going in one direction than in the other.

Over-bent – Describes the horse's head when positioned beyond the vertical towards the chest.

Nap – A horse who either from stubbornness or bad temper refuses to carry out the wishes of his rider, i.e. refusing to leave the yard, or other horses etc.

Neck-strap – a circular leather strap worn around the neck through which the martingale is passed and held in place.

Passage – An advanced dressage movement comprising an elevated trot in slow motion with a definite period of suspension as each pair of diagonal legs are lifted off the ground.

Piaffe – Similar to the above but without any forward movement.

Pirouette – An advanced dressage movement in which the horse pivots on his hindlegs, the forelegs executing a complete circle around them.

Pommel – The front of the saddle.

Port – An arc in the center of the mouthpiece of a straight bar bit – the higher the port the greater the bit's severity.

Runs up light – A horse that, because of slackness over his loins and a marked space between the last rib and hip bone, loses condition after work so he resembles a greyhound.

Surcingle – A wide strap, usually sewn onto a rug to keep it in place.

Tack-up – To put on the saddle and bridle.

Under saddle – Being ridden.

Unschooled – A horse that has not been trained for the purpose required.

Weaving – A stable vice of nervous origin where the horse transfers his weight from one foot to another and weaves his head back and forth over the lower half of the stable door.

Index

aids 74, 78, 79, 83, 89, 95, 96, 98; artificial 89; Western 107
airs above the ground 182-3, *183*, 187
Akhal-Tekes 29, 48
Andalusians *see* Barbs
anemia 125
Anglo-Arabs 29
Appaloosas 33, *33*
Arabs 29, 32, 34, 37, 41, 45, 48, 105, 144; endurance riding 157; keeping 109; overall description 29; showing 159
Ardennais horses 41
ascarids *see* worms (white)

backing 81, 82
Badminton 155, 170, *170*, 174
barbed wire 109, *109*, *127*
Barbs, Spanish (Andalusians) 20, 21, *21*, *26*, 45, *45*, 105, 144
barrel racing 107
Bashkirs 48
Beaufort, 10th Duke of 155, 170
bedding 112, 114, *114*, *115*
Belgian Ardennes horses 41, *41*, 137
Ben Arthur 168, *169*, 171, *171*, 172
bitless bridles (bosals; hackamores) 61, 63, *63*, 105
bits 61-3, *62*, 70, 79, 91; ill fitting 128; Western 106, *106*
blankets 71-2, 105, *107*
blinkers 64
boots 72, *72*, 80
bosals *see* bitless bits
Boulonnais horses 41
boxes 112-13, *113*, *114*
branding *18*, 140, 186; *see also* freeze -branding
breastplates *67*, *188*
breeds 29-49, *29-35*, *37-8*, *40-41*, *43*, *45-6*, *48*; ancient 17; cold bloods 29; hot bloods 29; warm bloods 29, 30, 42
Breton horses 41
bridles *60*, 61-5, *62*, *63*; bridling 90, 91, *91*; dismantling 70; parts *68*; Western 105, 106, *106*
bridoons *62*; *see also* snaffle bits
bronco riding 161, *161*
browbands 64
Brumbies 25, *25*, 26
brushes, brushing 116, *116*, 117
brushing boots 72
Budenny horses 48
bullfighting *24*, 40, 45, 161

Calgary Stampede 161, *161*
Californian style 107
Camargue ponies 22, 24, *24*, 40, *40*
cannon bones 57, 58, 130
cantering *87*, 96, *97*, 101, 155

capriole 182, 183, 187
care (general) 109-21
cavalletti *80*, *82*, 84, 101-102, *101*
cavalry 66, 142, 155
cavessons *see* lunge cavessons
Championnat du Cheval d'Armes 155
chaps 107
Charisma 168, 170, 172, *174*, 175
cheekpieces (cheekstraps) 64, 79
chuck-wagon racing 161, *161*
cinches *see* girths
circuses 144, *144*
Cleveland Bays 30
clipping 110, 118, *118*
clothing, horses' 71-2
Clydesdale horses 38, 137, 145
coat *120*, 123, *123*, 125
colic 110, 125, 132
combined training 156, *156*; *see also* eventing
combs 117, *118*
conformation 56, 57-8, *58*
Connemaras 21, *21*, 22, 38, *38*
Corlay horses 41
corns 131
coughs 132
counter canter 155
courbette 182, 183, 187
cowboys 105, 106
cow horses (cow ponies) 140
cracked heels 57, 132
cross-country 74, *87*, 155, *155*, *156*, 166, *170*, 172, *172*; driving 156; jumping 152, 168, 170; *see also* speed-and-endurance tests
croup 58, 90
crownpieces 64
cruppers 81
curb bits *see* Pelham bits
curb chains *60*, 62, 65
curry combs 117, *118*

Dales ponies 21, 22, 26-27, 36
Dartmoor ponies 21, 22, 37, *37*
de Nemethy, Bert 163, 165, 166, 172
digestive complaints 132; *see also* colic
disease, signs of *122*, 123-4
dismounting 90, 94, *94*
distance poles *85*, 102
domestication 12-14, 19
Dons 48
double (Weymouth) bridles 61, 62, 63, 65
Draught Breton horses 41
draught (heavy) horses 38 , *38*, 41, 137-40
dressage 42, 48, 62, 107, *155*; ancient 14; driving 156; Grand Prix 155, 174; international 155, 168, 171; Olympic 174; training for 74
dressage saddles *67*, *67*
driving 156, *156*

drop nosebands 61, 64, *64*, 65
Dulmens 24, *24*
Dutch Draught horses 41

Eclipse line 30
education: of horses *see* training; of riders *see* teaching the rider
electric fencing 109
endurance riding 155, *156*, 157
English seat 66, 105
Eohippus (Hyracotherium) 9, 11
equipment (harness; tack) *60*, 61-73, *61-7*, *69-73*; cleaning 70, *70*; dirty 70, 128, *128*; Western *104*, 105-107, *105-107*; *see also individual items of tack*
Equus 9; *E. cabullus* 11, 12; *E. przewalskii see* Przewalski's Horse
eventing (combined training) 40, 42, 53; international 155; Olympic *166*, 168-9, 170, *171*, 174, *176*; three-day 155, 156, *156*, 166, *166*, 168-9, 170, *170*, *171*, *176*; training for 74, *74*
exercising *97*, 98, *98*, 112
Exmoor ponies (Celtic ponies) 21, 22, *22*, 23, 27, 36, 37, *37*
eyes 57, 123

Fargis, Joe 163, 175
Fédération Équestre Internationale 153
feed, feeding 54, 112, 114, 120, *120*, 132; bulk 120; hard concentrate 110, 120, *189*; rejection of 123; supplementary *115*; *see also* grass; hay
feet: checking *118*, *119*; evolution 11; ideal 58; picking out 110, 114, *116*, 117; problems 57, 128, 130-31, *131*, 132; wounds 127; *see also* lameness; shoes
Fell ponies 21, 22, 36
fences (jumps)) 84, *84*, *85*, 86, 101-102; show-jumping 152, 153
fencing 109, *109*, *127*
fetlocks 57
first aid 126-7
flash nosebands 63, 64, 75
flat racing 31, 147-8, *149*
flies *110*, 112
flying changes 107, 182, 187
foal slips 76-7
forward seat 66
freeze-branding 109, *109*
French Saddle horses *see* Selle Français horses
French Trotters 29, 40, 149
Friesian horses 22, 36, 42, 45
frog *116*, 130, 131

gags 61, *62*, 63
galling 70, 128, *128*

Gelderland horses 45, *45*
geldings 54
girths (cinches) 68, 70, *90*, 91, 92; adjusting 94; Western 105, 106
going forward 79
grass 109, 110, 120, 125
Green, Lucinda 170, 172, *172*
grooming 71, 79, 110, 112, 116-17, *116-18*
gymkhanas 147, 159

hackamores *see* bitless bridles
Haflinger horses 43, *43*, *133*, 144
half-breeds 29, 53
halt (stop) 102, 107
halters 71, 76-7, 78, 91
Hanoverians 42, *43*, 48
harness racing 148-9, *149*
haute école 180, 181-7, *181*, *183-4*, 187
hay 110, 113, 114, *115*, 120, *120*; dusty 132
haynets 110, 113, 114, *120*
hayracks 110, 113, *113*
headcollars 71, 78, 91
headpieces 64, 79, 91
health, signs of *120*, *122*, 123-4, *123*
Herod line 30
Hickstead 166, *166*
high collection 90
Highland ponies 21, 22, 35, *35*
hock boots 72
hocks 58, *58*
Holgate, Virginia 172, 176, *176*
Holstein horses 42, 45
Homfeld, Conrad 163, 175
hooves *116*, 117, 118, *131*
horse shows 105, 107, 158-9
horse trials 74
hunting 61, *146*, 151, 152, 166
hunt seat 158, 159
Hyracotherium see Eohippus

Icelandic ponies 23, 46, *46*
illness, behavior in 124; *see also* medical care
impulsion 89
"in balance" 89, 90, 101
inflammations 123, 130, 132
influenza 59, 124
in-hand walking 76, 79, 80
injuries 127, *127-9*
inoculations *see* vaccinations
Irish Draughts 30

jaundice 123
Jockey Club 147, 151
jumper's bump 58
jumping 57, 66, 159; learning 82, 84, *84*, *85*, *85*, 86, 101-102, *101*, *102*; *see also* show jumping
jumping saddles 67

Karabairs 48
Kentucky Saddlers *see* Saddlebreds
kidney trouble 123

Klimke, Reiner 174, *174*, 176
Knabstrupers 144
knee pads 72
knees, broken 127

lameness *57*, 58, 128-31, 131; intermittent 128-31
laminitis 130, 131, *131*
Latvian Riding horses 48
leading 79, 80, 92
leg protectors 72, *72*
legs 57-8, 123; problems *127*, 130-31, 132; resting 123; wounds 127; *see also* feet; lameness
levade *181*, 182-3, 187, *187*
lice 123
Lipizza, stud at 184, 186
Lipizzaner horses 26, 45, *45*, 144, *180*, 181-7 *passim*, *184*, *187*
lip straps *60*, 62, 65
liveries 54
long-distance riding *see* endurance riding
lunge cavessons *77*, 78, *78*, *79*, 81, 82, 83
lungeing *77*, 78-81, *78*, *79*, 82-3, 98, 182
lunge reins 78-9, 80, 81
lung infections 132
Lusitano horses 45

malnutrition 123
mane 117, *117*
martingales (tie-downs) *64*, 65, *65*, 89
Matchem line 30
medical care *122*, 123-33, *123-4*, *127-32*; preventive 124-5
Mergels 48
midges 132
mineral licks 110
monkey seat 149
Moorland ponies *35*, 159
Morgans 29, 31, 32, *32*, 141
Mountain ponies *35*, 159
mounting 68, 82, 90, 92-4, *92*
mouth sores 128
mucking-out 112, 114, *114*, *115*
mud fever 132
Mustangs *19*, 20-21, 27, 105

Narragansett Pacers 31, 32
navicular disease 128, 131
neck reining 107
nerve blocks 128
New Forest ponies 21, *21*, 22, *37*, *37*, *108*
New Zealand rugs 71, *71*, 110, 118
Norfolk Roadsters 41
Norwegian Fjords 46, *46*
nose, 57, 123
nosebands 61, *63*, 64, *64*, 91
numnahs (saddle pads) 69, *69*

obstacle driving 156
Oldenburgs 29, 42, 45
Olympic Games 155, 156, 163-77, *163-76*; Gold Medalists

179; "substitute" (Fontainebleau, 1980) 176
Orlov Trotters 29, 48, *48*, 149
over-reach boots 72, *72*
over-reaches 127

pacing 148, 149, *149*
palominos *104*
parade horses 33, 138, 141
Pas de Deux *183*, 187
passage 90, 155, 182, 187
passing-gaited trotters 31
pasterns 57, *129*
pato 161
pattern shoes 131
Peacock irons 68, 69
Pelham (curb) bits *60*, 61, 62, 63, 65
Percherons 29, 41, *41*, 137, *139*
piaffe 90, 155, 182, 187
Piber *26*, *180*, 184, *184*, 186
pillars, between 182, *183*, 187
pirouette 182, 183, 187
pivots 107
pneumonia 132
point-to-point *146*, 151, 152
poisonous plants 109
police horses *140*, 141
pollguards *73*
polo 158, *158*
pommels 66, 67, 91, 105
Postier horses 41
posting trot *see* rising trot
pounding races 150
presentation (in driving) 156
Prix de l'Arc de Triomphe 148
Prix des Nations 163, 165
Przewalski's Horse (*Equus Przewalskii*) 10, 12, 17, 24
pulse 124, 132

Quarter Horses 29, 33, 140

racecourses (racetracks) 147
racing 29, *30*, 33, 48, 147-51, *147*, *149*, *151*; barrel 107; chuck-wagon 161, *161*; pounding 150; *see also different types of racing*
racing saddles 67
racing seat 149
rack 31
rein-back 102
reins 91, 92, 94; for different bridle-types *60*, 62, 63, 64-5; long 81, *183*; side *79*, 81, 84; Western 107; *see also* lunge reins
respiration 124, 125, 132
ringbones 130
ringworm 132
rising (posting) trot 94-5, *95*, 101
rodeos 33, 105, 161, *161*
rollers *77*, *79*, 81, *128*
roping *104*, 106, 107, 161, *161*
roundings 63
rubbing 128
rubbing cloths/pads (wisps) 117
rugs 71-2, *71*, 114

Saddlebreds 31, *31*, 159
saddle (side) flaps 94, 105
saddle horns 106
saddle pads *see* numnahs
saddles: dressage 67, *67*; parts 68; repair costs 54; saddling 90, *90*, 91; Spanish 105; stripping 70; types 66-9, *69*; Western 105, *105*, 106, *107*
saddle seat 158, 159
saddle sores 128, *128*
saddle trees 67, *69*
saddling up 82, *90*
salt licks 110
salts 120
Sardinian wild horses 24
Schockemöhle, Alwin 165, *165*
schooling 62, 98, 102, 187
School Quadrille 181, *181*, *184*, 187
scratching 76
seat 66, 90, 94, *95*, *97*, 98, *98*, 102, 149, 158; Western 106, 107
Selle Français horses (French Saddle horses) 29, 30, 40, *40*, 166, *166*
shelter 110-12, *110*
Shetland ponies 21, 22, 23, 35, *35*, 144
Shire horses 29, 38, *38*, *136*, 137, 138, *139*
shoes, shoeing 54, 71, 76, *116*, 117, 118, *118*, 119, 128; corrective 131, *131*
showing 31, 53, 54, 158-9, *158*
show jumping 29, 40, 42, 48, 53, 147, *152*, *153*, 155, 156; international 153; Olympic 163-6, *163*, 168, *171*, *176*; training for 74
sitting trot 98, *98*, 101
skin diseases 132
skirts *see* saddle (side) flaps
Sloan, Todhunter 149
sloping seat 106
Smith, Harvey 165
Smith, Melanie *163*, 165, *176*
snaffle bits 61, *61*, 62, 63
spade bits 105, *106*
Spanish Riding School *26*, 45, *45*, *180*, 181-7, *181*, *183-4*, *187*
spavins 130, 131
speed-and-endurance tests *166*, 168, 172
"splints" 130
sporting horses 137, *146*, 147-77, *147-77 passim*
spurs 89, 107
stable management *see* care (general)
stabling 112-13
Standardbreds 29, 30, 31, *31*; racing 148, 149
staring coat 120, 123, 125
steeplechasing *146*, *149*, 150-51, *151*, 152, 155, 168
stirrup bars 67
stirrup irons 68-9, *70*, 91, 92
stirrup leathers 67, 68, 70, 91; adjusting 94; Western 105, *105*, 106

stirrup pads 69
stirrups 66, 105; forgoing 98
stitching (suturing) 127, *129*
Stives, Karen 168, *169*, 171, *171*, 172, 176
stock seat 158, 159
stop *see* halt
strains 130, 131
straw 113, 114, *115*
striking-off 96
strongyles *see* worms (red)
Suffolks 38, 137
suppleness exercises 86-7, *97*, *98*
surcingles 71, *128*
Swedish Warm Bloods 46
sweet itch 132, *132*

tack *see* equipment
tacking up 90, 91-4
tail 72, *116*, 117, *117*, *132*
tail bandages 72, 117
teaching the rider *88*, 89-103, *89-107*
teeth 78; fossil 9; problems 123, *124*, 125
temperature 124, 132
tendon boots 72
tendons 130, 131
Tennessee Walking horses 32, 159
tetanus (lock-jaw) 59, 124, *124*, 127
Texan style 107
Thoroughbreds 29, *30*, 31, 33, 34, 37, 40, 42, 45, 48, 53, 141; keeping 109; Olympic 163; overall description 30; racing 148
three-quarter-breeds 29
throatlatches (throatlashes) 64, *69*, 91, *91*
thrush 130
tie-downs *see* martingales
Todd, Mark 168, 170, *174*, 175
training 74-87, *74*, *76-80*, *82*, *84-5*, *87*; cavalry 155; *haute école* 182; movies 143; nursery stage 74, 76-7, *76*; police 141; primary 74, *77*, 78-85, *78-80*, *82*, *84-5*; secondary 74, 85-7, *87*
Trakehners (East Prussians) 30, 42
traveling 54, 71, 76
traveling boots 72
trees *see* saddle trees
trotting *89*, 94-5, *95*, *98*
trotting races 31, 45, 148, 149, *149*

Ukrainians 48
ultra-sonic therapy 127, *127*
urine 123

vaccinations (inoculations) 59, 124, *124*
vitamins 120

walking 76, *79*, 94-5
warbles 132

warhorses 142
water, watering 110, *110*, 112, 113, *113*, 114
water jumps 153
Welsh Cobs 32, 34
Welsh Mountain ponies 21, 22, *22*, 29, 34
Welsh ponies 34, 144
Welsh Ponies of Cob Type 34
Western riding *104*, 105-107;

horse shows 158, 159
whips 79, 80, 83, 89
wild horses *10*, *18*, 19-27, *19-22*, *24-6*
wind, broken 132
Windsor grays *136*
Winkler, Hans Günter 42, 166, 174
withers 57, 58
wolf teeth 125

working horses 29, 38, *136*, 137-45, *139-40*, *143-5*
World Championships 42, 156, 163, 166, 170, 171, 172; Women's 166
worms, worming 109, 110, 123, 125, 132; red 125; white 125
wounds 127, *127-9*; deep 127; puncture 127

PICTURE CREDITS

Allsport Photographic 172, 174-178 **J G Baker** 17 **Gerry Cranham** 163-166 **Daily Telegraph** 137 **Robert Estall** 12 **Sonia Halliday** 8, 16 bottom **Robert Harding** 24 bottom **Kit Houghton** 21 bottom left, 162, 171, 173 **The Kobal Collection** 143 bottom **Frank Lane** 6-7, 139 top **Bob Languish** 18, 26, 31, 32, 37 top, 40 top, 41, 42, 50-51, 136, 138, 140, 145 top, 146, 147, 150, 151, 155-157, 161 top, 167, 168-169, 186 **Van Phillips** 28 **Mike Roberts** 22, 141, 142, 143 top, 148 **Peter Roberts** contents, 10, 16 top, 21 bottom right, 33, 37 bottom, 52, 57 top right, 59-74, 77-132, 134-135, 139 centre and bottom, 144, 145 bottom, 152-154, 158-160, 161 bottom, 170, 181-183, 185 **Ronald Sheridan** 11, 13-15 **Sally Anne Thompson** 35, 36, 38, 44, 46, 47, 184 **Zefa** title, half title, endpapers, 19, 20, 21 top right, 23, 24 top, 25, 27, 29, 30, 39, 40 bottom, 43, 45, 76, 133, 180.

Illustrations by James Marffy

Multimedia Publications (UK) Limited have endeavoured to observe the legal requirements with regard to the suppliers of photographic and illustrative materials.